CÉCILE DUBOIS

BRUSSELS ART DECO

PHOTOS | SOPHIE VOITURON

WALKING
IN THE CITY CENTRE

CÉCILE DUBOIS

BRUSSELS ART DECO

PHOTOS | SOPHIE VOITURON

LANNOO

INTRODUCTION

At the end of the nineteenth century, architects in Brussels turned to Art Nouveau as a reaction against academic art. Victor Horta, with his organic style, and Paul Hankar, with his more geometric style, created a new architectural language, which soon became internationally famous, earning Brussels the title of European Art Nouveau Capital to this day.

Art Nouveau, meaning "new art", was a fleeting moment in art history, lasting just over ten years and falling out of favour just before World War I. There were two dominant architectural styles during the interwar period in Brussels, which existed alongside one another, with multiple variations, i.e., Art Deco and Modernism.

Without aspiring to be exhaustive, this book aims to give an overview of Brussels architecture during the Twenties and Thirties, while examining some of the issues associated with these styles and the work of a few prominent architects in further detail.

◂ Ciamberlani House,
48 rue Defacqz, Ixelles, arch. Paul Hankar, 1897

BELGIAN SOCIETY DURING THE INTERWAR PERIOD

By the end of World War I, which was a conflict with an unimaginable scope, the population was impatient for normal life to resume. Life would never be the same, however, and a new society emerged, which was defined for two decades by contradictory influences, including social progress, economic crises, prosperity for some and misery for others...

In 1919, universal suffrage for men, which was already a topic before the war, was finally enacted, changing the political landscape. While women had a lot more freedom compared with before the war, they could still only vote in municipal elections.

The Catholics lost the majority which they had held since 1884 as a result of this universal suffrage, forcing them to form coalitions with the liberals and the socialists. Belgium had eighteen governments in all during the years from 1918 until 1940, which were forced to deal with various crises associated with monetary instability, language issues, the need for social reform and so on.

The authorities promptly took measures to eliminate social equality and improve the living conditions of workers, limiting working time to 48 hours a week and 8 hours a day, enacting the right to strike and the freedom of association as well as 6 days of leave per year, compulsory insurance against unemployment, sickness and disability...

The way of working also changed, both in factories and in offices. No effort was spared to make operations more rational, better organised and more efficient, resulting in increased mechanisation, assembly line production, bigger companies and the dehumanisation of workers and employees as well as giving rise to new relations with employers. Films like Fritz Lang's *Metropolis* (1927) or Charlie Chaplin's *Modern Times* (1936) paint a rather caricatural picture of these situations.

The government also had to focus on other greater issues, namely rebuilding a country that had been devastated by war and a lack of affordable housing. In 1919, the *Société nationale des habitations et logements à bon marché* (The National Affordable Housing Society) was established to promote the construction of housing. The succession of monetary and economic crises was also a problem. The international crisis, which kicked off with the crash of the New York Stock Exchange in 1929, also affected Belgium, culminating in various social problems, such as rising unemployment, declining purchasing power, strikes... The authorities launched a series of large-scale construction projects in an attempt to alleviate the problems, as construction sites employed a lot of workers. One such example is the resumption of the work on the North-South connection in Brussels. In the face of all these economic and social problems, as well as the international situation which clearly was a harbinger of a new imminent conflict, the population was easily tempted by extremist movements with a populist message.

DAILY LIFE DURING THE INTERWAR PERIOD

In spite of all these problems, the population's daily life vastly improved during the interwar period. The standard of healthcare, education and housing was better. Once peace was re-established, the population indulged in the pleasures that were available to it. Monetary instability prompted people to live in the here and now, to consume and to live life to the full. These were the decades of jazz, tango, and popular music. Everyone could afford a cinema ticket and many new cinemas sprung up, especially in Brussels. America was regarded as a cultural reference and music hall was a huge success. The first jazz bands were formed and soon every music hall wanted to have its own jazz band. The performance of Josephine Baker and the *Revue nègre* in Brussels in 1925 was the highlight of the year. The population, which now had more free time, flocked to sports events. Boxing, cycling and football were the most popular pastimes and sports halls and stadiums were built that were big enough to accommodate the masses on Sunday afternoons.

Fashion, especially women's fashion, soon adapted to the new lifestyles. Gone were the corsets and the long dresses in heavy fabrics. Modern women preferred to wear lighter clothes, which also contributed to their gradual emancipation. The *garçonne*, or flapper, with her short hair, cigarette holder, bowler hat or beret, was the epitome of the liberated woman of the Twenties. Thanks to technological progress, soon every woman could afford fashionable clothes and cosmetics.

Cars became faster, more comfortable and safer and were soon built on assembly lines. The railway network was expanded and steam engines made way for diesel and even electric locomotives. Ocean liners continued

▼ Dining room of the D. and A. van Buuren Museum, 41, av. Léo Errera, Uccle, 1924-1928

to cross the Atlantic but soon had to compete with civil aviation. People also flocked to air shows.
Homes also became more comfortable. Of course, only the rich could afford to hire interior designers but gradually the authorities also paid more attention to ensuring working-class homes had the basic amenities. While fitted kitchens and bathrooms were not the norm for everyone, worker's dwellings now had running water, their own WC and in most cases, electricity.
The attraction to speed and this new lifestyle was fuelled by advertising in newspapers and on the radio, two fast-developing media.

THE EMERGENCE OF ART DECO AND MODERNISM

Architecture also experienced a revival with the emergence of Art Deco and Modernism. Art Deco prolonged the decorative vein of Art Nouveau, albeit it with a purer and more geometric aesthetic, with the repetition of geometric and stylised motifs and the use of traditional and modern materials. Modernism, by contrast, sought to ban all ornamentation and any reference to older styles. Distinguishing between modernist and Art Deco designs is sometimes difficult, as is categorising the work of an architect or a specific building... As Patrick Burniat reminds us, *you cannot overlook the cross-pollination between two extremes: the romantic Modernism of an architect like Pompe, Verbruggen's more attenuated Modernism and the refined Art Deco of Diongre, all styles which are considered to be innovative. At the same time, you cannot overlook the work of radicals like Louis Herman De Koninck, who created Art Deco style designs at one time or another in their career. Beyond the stylistic aspect, the traces of modernity are also, or even mainly, apparent in their innovative approach to space, in their desire to build functional and comfortable houses, in their transformation of the relationship between the interior and the exterior, their use of new materials and techniques, the wider adaptation of dwellings to new social demands, the designer's intentions, and so on.*[1]
The architects of this period were subjected to various influences. They were all influenced by the construction, in 1905-1911, of the Stoclet Palace (279-281, av. de Tervueren, Woluwe-Saint-Pierre). This mansion, which was built by the Austrian architect Josef Hoffmann, introduced Brussels to the Viennese Secession, an Austrian variant of Art Nouveau, the shapes of which already heralded Art Deco. This gesamtkunstwerk was decorated by the Wiener Werkstätte, the artists of the Viennese workshops. The building's simplicity, its cube volumes, the division of its window frames into smaller squares, the emphasising of its edges, its graphic black and white design, the repetition of stylised motifs... were all very novel and surprising. Another influence was Dutch architecture. Because of their proximity to the Netherlands, many young Belgian architects were aware of the work of their Dutch counterparts. Many architects also fled to the Netherlands during World War I, participating in the reflection on the reconstruction of Belgium after the war. The Amsterdam School had a strong influence on Art Deco and Modernist architects while De Stijl inspired the more radical Modernists.
The Belgian architects adopted the principles of Expressionist effects, which were achieved by arranging the bricks in geometric and relief patterns, from the Amsterdam School, a group of architects and designers who worked in this style from 1915 until 1930. From the De Stijl movement (1917-1928), around the painter Piet Mondrian, they retained the idea of structures made up of simple rectangular brick or concrete blocks which were not decorated, except with (primary) colour accents. The combination of the volumes added depth and relief. Some Belgian architects also believed, in line with these two movements, that the world could be transformed through architecture, if even the simplest and most economical programmes, such as working-class apartment buildings,

▲ Stoclet Palace, 279-281, av. de Tervueren, Woluwe-Saint-Pierre, arch. J. Hoffmann, 1905-1911

had an element of dignity to them. The Dutch architect H.P. Berlage (1856-1934), who championed a social approach to architecture and who was an early Modernist, also inspires various Belgian architects, as did the American architect Frank Lloyd Wright (1867-1959), whose influence is apparent in the Art Deco designs of Victor Horta and Antoine Courtens and in Lucien François's Modernist designs.

ART DECO AND MODERNISM BECOME A PERMANENT FIXTURE

The influence of Art Deco and Modernism continued after the interwar period. Even today Art Deco continues to inspire many designers and architects. Modernism was also used in large complexes and large-scale operations. The inhumanity of these signs soon became apparent, when Modernist principles were only applied for money-saving purposes, therefore losing their poetic dimension.

ART DECO

The term Art Deco was coined in 1968, in a publication by the British historian Bevis Hillier, titled *Art Deco of the 20s and 30s*, which refers to the International Exhibition of Modern Decorative and Industrial Arts, which was held in 1925. This provided a unique opportunity for architects and the public to become acquainted with this new mindset and style. Art Deco's eclecticism became apparent in the way it borrowed from other styles, other cultures like Egypt, Pompeii, Assyria... In Belgium, the Congo was an inexhaustible treasure trove of exotic influences. The architecture of the ocean liners was also very inspiring, both for architects and designers.

Art Deco influenced both architecture and the decorative arts, cultivating an appetite for aspirations and luxury, while also relying on mass production and cheap everyday objects. The style expressed the ambitions of a generation that was interested in breaking

▾ Villa Empain / Boghossian Foundation, 67, av. F. Roosevelt, Brussels, arch. M. Polak, 1930-1934

with the past and living in the moment. The broken, geometric lines conveyed speed, lightning, mechanical movements and are typical of this era.

MODERNISM

Like Art Deco, Modernism had its roots in pre-war designs. An architect like Fernand Bodson already argued in favour of a more rational approach to architecture at the time, stripped of the notion of style, and expressing more democratic ideals. In 1910, Antoine Pompe built a clinic for Dr Van Neck in Saint-Gilles. All the decorative effects were dictated by functional or constructive necessity. The early Modernists did not reject ornamentation per se but felt that it should be a natural consequence of the building's structure. They used brick and continued to build gabled roofs. This generation of Modernists, which included Antoine Pompe and Fernand Bodson, was very different from the second generation of architects, led by Victor Bourgeois and Louis Herman De Koninck among others, who were initially inspired by the ideas from the Bauhaus in Germany and the Dutch De Stijl movement. Later, they were influenced by the theories of Le Corbusier, defending an architecture without any ornamentation or style references, which expressed the building's function and the constructive techniques that were used. The second generation outclassed the first generation until 1969, when Archives d'Architecture moderne organised an exhibition titled *Antoine Pompe and the modern effort in Belgium.* The exhibition provided a unique opportunity to rediscover the fundamental role the first generation of modernists had played and highlighted the poetic dimension of their designs. Unlike Art Deco, Modernism had a more ideological slant, proposing to change society. These considerations aroused the mistrust of individuals and the authorities, who chose not to work with them on larger projects, forcing them to design private houses for the most part. The Modernists did, however, participate in the many theoretical reflections on the organisation of cities. They published extensively, in the many journals that were on the market at the time, organised exhibitions, talks and visits and attended international conferences. Many of them were also able to transmit their ideas through education, teaching at the La Cambre National School of Decorative Arts.

▼ Dr Van Neck's clinic, 53, rue Waefelaerts, Saint-Gilles, arch. A. Pompe, 1910

LE CORBUSIER'S INFLUENCE

The fascination for the Swiss-born French architect Le Corbusier (1887-1965) was evident from the Thirties onwards. The architect's concept of a house as a machine for living as a solution to the housing problem influenced thinking about housing and architecture. It was implemented on a larger scale after World War II in such projects like the Model City (1955-1974, Laeken). Le Corbusier championed the idea of building standardised high-rises with apartments in them. He was able to experiment with his ideas in the apartment buildings he built in France in the Fifties and Sixties. These vertical garden cities, with several hundreds of standardised duplex apartments, also offered a wide range of amenities: a library, a nursery, shops... Architects in Brussels were however influenced by Le Corbusier's Five Points of Architects rather than by his machine-for-living concept. The five principles, which he developed in 1927, are

1. building on *pilotis*, or reinforced concrete columns (the building no longer rests on the ground, the garden extends under the building),
2. the roof-garden (to be used as a sun terrace),
3. the free design of the ground plan (the elimination of supporting walls using new reinforced concrete structures to open up the space, meaning the structure no longer influences the ground plan),
4. the horizontal window (for maximum daylight) and
5. the free design of the façade (as the façade is no longer load-bearing, it becomes a slim envelope of the building, with light walls and windows).

Belgian followers of Le Corbusier include Paul-Amaury Michel, Émile Goffay and Marcel Leborgne who built the Villa Dirickx in Rhode-Saint-Genèse in 1933.
Its façade is flanked by an external spiral staircase which connects the ground floor with the roof terrace. Belgian Modernists were quick to pick up on the idea of building duplexes, after seeing some of Le Corbusier's

▼ Villa Dirickx, 28, av. Marie-Jeanne, Rhode-Saint-Genèse, arch. M. Leborgne, 1933

creations. The duplex was fronted by a large slab of glass and had the advantage of creating interesting interior perspectives.
Unfortunately Modernists rarely thought of the long-term and the maintenance of their designs. Reinforced concrete, which was still an experimental material at the time, suffered in the Belgian climate. As a result, many of the roof terraces leaked and the metal frames caused insulation problems. This explains why so many of the Modernist designs fell into disrepair so soon after they were built...

THE CIAM CONGRESSES

Modern architecture was also inspired by the meetings between architects at the end of the Twenties and throughout the Thirties. Le Corbusier took the initiative for the International Congresses of Modern Architecture or CIAM, which were organised on ten occasions in the period from 1928 until 1956. They provided a platform for architects to meet and discuss specific topics. The third congress was held in Brussels, at the suggestion of Victor Bourgeois and discussed rational subdivision (1930).
The fourth congress was held on a ship bound for Athens in 1933. During the conference, the participants drafted the Athens Charter, which was regarded as the bible of contemporary urban planning for many years. It advocated an urban planning based on four separate human functions, to be harmoniously developed in the modern city, i.e., living, working, recreation and traffic.
In some cases, the application of these principles gave rise to excesses and the creation of monofunctional neighbourhoods. Over time, it became clear that this was not a good solution from an urban planning perspective. After World War II, this gave rise to the construction in Brussels of the State's Administrative City (1955-1980) and the Model City.

PROGRAMMES AND LOCATION IN BRUSSELS

Brussels has several interwar designs, with different programmes: luxury apartment buildings, private dwellings, villas, working-class homes, garden cities, offices, cinemas, cafés and hotels, hospitals, schools, railway stations, shops... The city centre is dotted with apartment buildings from this period, which replaced older buildings, or were built on vacant lots. The architectural ensembles of the interwar period are located in the municipalities of the second tier, i.e., the municipalities that do not directly adjoin the Pentagon and which were not densely built up in the early Twenties. These include Uccle, Forest, parts of Ixelles and Molenbeek...

This guide features a selection of neighbourhoods with significant designs, which can be visited on foot or by bike. Tours of the Quartier des Fleurs or the Quartier des Pierres Précieuses in Schaerbeek, Woluwe-Saint-Pierre or Woluwe-Saint-Lambert could provide material for future publications. The Heysel plateau in Laeken is also very interesting because it was designed for the 1935 Brussels International Exposition and was subsequently used for the Brussels World Fair, also known as Expo 1958.

ABBREVIATIONS

AAM Modern Architecture Archives / Archives d'Architecture moderne

arch. architect

AVB Archives of the City of Brussels / Archives de la Ville de Bruxelles

CGER Savings and pensions fund / Caisse générale d'Épargne et de Retraite

CIAM International Congresses of Modern Architecture / Congrès internationaux d'Architecture moderne

COGENI construction company / Compagnie générale d'Entreprise immobilière

CPAS Public social welfare centre / Centre public d'action (ou d'aide) sociale

ENSAV The La Cambre National School of Visual Arts / École nationale supérieure des Arts visuels (La Cambre)

ETRIMO construction company / Études et Réalisations immobilières

INR National Radio Broadcasting Institute / Institut national de la Radiodiffusion

SBI real estate company / Société belge immobilière

SNHLBM National affordable housing society / Société nationale des habitations et logements à bon marché

TP Civil engineering / Travaux publics

ULB Université libre de Bruxelles

▸ Stoclet Palace, 279-281, av. de Tervueren, Woluwe-Saint-Pierre, arch. J. Hoffmann, 1905-1911

FIRST WALK

THE IXELLES PONDS AND AVENUE ROOSEVELT

LA LOGE TO VILLA EMPAIN

From the old location of the Masonic Lodge to Villa Empain, we will discover some architectural gems from the interwar period, including apartment buildings, town houses, cultural institutions, schools... This rather long walk can be taken in one go or split in two. The first part of the walk connects La Loge to Rond-Point de l'Etoile, by way of Flagey and the Ixelles Ponds. The second part continues along avenue Roosevelt, to Villa Empain, where the Boghossian Foundation is now located. This art centre aims to promote a dialogue between the cultures of the east and west.

◄ Rear view, Villa Empain / Fondation Boghossian, av. Roosevelt 67

rue de l'Ermitage
chée d'Ixelles
place Flagey
avenue Louise
chaussée de Vleurgat
avenue Général De Gaulle
avenue de l'Hippodrome
boulevard Général Jacques
ave E. Duray
Abbaye de
la Cambre
rond-point
de l'Etoile
avenue Franklin Roosevelt
chaussée de Waterloo
avenue Jeanne
ULB
Cimetière d'Ixelles
avenue Antoine Depage
square
du Solbosch
avenue de l'Orée
ave des Phalènes
Bois de
la Cambre
avenue Victoria
ave des Scarabées
avenue Franklin Roosevelt
avenue du Brésil
station Villo
1
2
3
4
5
6
7
8
9
10
11
12
13
14
15
16

01 FORMER MASONIC LODGE
86, rue de l'Ermitage, 1050 Ixelles

02 APARTMENT BUILDING
28, rue de l'Ermitage, 1050 Ixelles

03 FORMER RADIO BROADCASTING INSTITUTE
18, place Eugène Flagey, 1050 Ixelles

04 LA CASCADE
36, avenue Général De Gaulle, 1050 Ixelles

05 RÉSIDENCE BELLE-VUE
50, avenue Général de Gaulle, 1050 Ixelles

06 LE TONNEAU
51, avenue Général de Gaulle, 1050 Ixelles

07 GROUP OF DWELLINGS
1-27, square du Val de la Cambre, 1050 Ixelles

08 PALAIS DE LA CAMBRE
60-68, avenue Émile Duray, 4, avenue de la Folle Chanson, 1050 Ixelles and Brussels

09 PALAIS DE LA FOLLE CHANSON
2, boulevard Général Jacques, 1050 Ixelles

10 RÉSIDENCE ERNESTINE
3, rond-point de l'Étoile, 1050 Ixelles

11 DOUBLE HÔTEL DE BODT
27-29, avenue Franklin Roosevelt, 1050 Brussels

12 PRIVATE HOME OF THE ARCHITECT AND APARTMENT BUILDING
52, avenue Franklin Roosevelt
and 1, avenue Antoine Depage, 1050 Brussels

13 PRIVATE DWELLING
90, avenue Franklin Roosevelt, 1050 Brussels

14 VILLA EMPAIN / FONDATION BOGHOSSIAN
67, avenue Franklin Roosevelt and 32, avenue Victoria, 1050 Brussels

15 APARTMENT BUILDING
4, avenue des Scarabées, 1050 Brussels

16 VILLA
3, avenue du Brésil, 1050 Brussels

1/ FORMER MASONIC LODGE

86, RUE DE L'ERMITAGE, 1050 IXELLES

Architects: Fernand Bodson and Louis Van Hooveld
Built: 1934-1935

This building, which was built for the Belgian Federation of Human Rights, originally only had a ground floor, where the temple was located, which was covered by a roof with a slight pitch and a small upper floor that was set back.

In 1955, the building was raised to accommodate a second temple and offices. This transformation is invisible as the same brick was used. In 1984, Droit humain moved out and the building was used by the Archives d'Architecture moderne as an archive centre. In 2001-2002, it became an architecture museum.

It currently is home to La Loge, a Brussels space dedicated to art and contemporary practices. The volumes and decoration of 1935 were preserved, including the large temple, a vast parallelepiped rectangle, that was painted white. From the outside, only the building's striking volumetry and its dark wooden entrance draw attention to this unassuming building. The porch is set in the façade and was the starting point of a symbolic journey from the shadows to the light. One of the first Modernist architects, Fernand Bodson (1877–1966) refused any references to older styles. At the same time, he never built extremely pared-down buildings. A committed philanthropist, who also founded several journals, he was involved in the discussions on the rebuilding of Belgium after the Great War. He built social housing and developed prefabrication methods. At the end of the Twenties, he distanced himself from the Modernist movement, despairing over its radicalism. He ended up moving to the United States. This voluntary exile also explains why he is not very well-known.

◀ Former Masonic Lodge

Also by Fernand Bodson, next to the former masonic lodge, at 2-4 rue Paul Spaak, this Modernist building (1930) was used by two artists, as a studio, each with its own skylight. The façade is clad with terracotta tiles, which accentuate the building's horizontal design. One of the two entrances leads to a courtyard, and an older house, where the Bodson family once lived. This building and the adjacent dwellings (6 and 8 were also designed by Bodson and date from 1927), which were built in the former location of an ice-house, and the first Decroly school attest to the huge talent of this architect.

CIVA, the international centre for city, architecture and landscape, is situated on the uneven side, in rue de l'Ermitage. On the even side, you will see a series of apartment buildings dating from the interwar period, after a group of more modern buildings that were built after World War II, where a V1 fell in 1944 (58 through 70). At No. 52, an Art Deco house (arch. Adolphe Puissant, 1923) with the original brick designs and stylised owls under the first-floor windows; at No. 50, an Art Deco apartment building with a distinctive entrance (arch. Jos Mouton, 1925) ; at No. 48, a modernist apartment building, built for the real estate developer Les Pavillons français (arch. Marcel Peeters, 1938) ; at No. 46, an apartment building which resembles an ocean liner, with an impressive volumetry (arch. Lucien De Vestel, 1936).

◀ Dwellings, 2-4, rue Paul Spaak, arch. F. Bodson

2/ APARTMENT BUILDING

28, RUE DE L'ERMITAGE, 1050 IXELLES

Architect: Louis Herman De Koninck
Built: 1935

The façade of this small modernist building, with five apartments, is made of a reinforced concrete wall, a technique which the architect developed and perfected. The span of the stairwell, which originally was much more refined and featured more subdivisions, has been altered. There was a small dwelling and an office for a liberal profession on the ground floor. On the upper floors, the luminous one-bedroom apartments had a balcony at the front and at the rear, with railings that were reminiscent of ocean liners. A staircase led from the balcony at the rear on the top floor to the rooftop terrace, with a canopy.

16, rue de l'Ermitage, a corner building (arch. Jos Mouton, 1925) stands out because of the vast terrace on the first floor, above the garages. Its concave façade, with white stone elements, brick combinations and protruding balconies must be seen from a distance. The entrance on the side has several stunning details, including the luminaire, the letterboxes, the boot scraper on a granito and stone floor...

◂ Apartment building,
16, rue de l'Ermitage, arch. J. Mouton

3/ FORMER RADIO BROADCASTING INSTITUTE

18, PLACE EUGÈNE FLAGEY, 1050 IXELLES

Architect: Joseph Diongre
Built: 1935-1938
Listed: 28/4/1994

The National Radio Broadcasting Institute (Institut national de la Radiodiffusion (INR)) was founded in 1930. It required a large building, for ten recording studios and offices, and a hall for the public. In 1933, the project of an architect called Diongre was selected for its technical and aesthetic properties, after a competition. This massive building, which was built between 1935 and 1938, inspired by ocean liners, is clad with yellow bricks. The horizontal windows, which are so typical of modernist architecture, add to the building's powerful horizontal appearance, which is offset by the verticality of the entrances (one for the public in place Sainte-Croix and the other for INR employees in place Flagey) and the corner turret for the TV antenna, which the architect sensed was the next step. The municipality of Ixelles required that the ground-floor be transformed into shops. The building fulfilled several technical requirements. The recording studios, which came in various sizes, were large enough for an audience and were situated in two acoustic towers with thick walls, which in a sense are the building's vertebral columns, around which the administrative and technical offices were built. The building's interior design and its furniture, its precious wood panelling and thick carpeting, were also created by Diongre. From the outset, this building became internationally famous for the quality of its studios, attracting world-class musicians. In 1953, the building also witnessed the advent of television. When the radio and TV broadcasting corporation left the premises in 1974, it was only sporadically used until it finally closed in 1995. Despite the fact that parts of it were listed, its future remained uncertain for quite some time due to the use of asbestos. In 1997, a working group of personalities from the private and arts sectors devised a plan to save the building and give it a new use. On 30 June 1998, the limited company Maison de la Radio Flagey acquired the building and undertook its restoration. Flagey reopened in October 2002. The entrance in place Sainte-Croix once again leads to the former studios, which now host cultural events. The entrance in place Flagey leads to the offices that are occupied by private companies. The Belga Café, the Variétés restaurant and the ticket office are located in the former shops. On the side of place Flagey, the adjoining building (No. 19) was built in the Fifties, in the same style as the IRN, taking into account the strict urban planning rules that apply to any building in the square.

▼ Former Radio Broadcasting Institute

4/ LA CASCADE

36, AVENUE GÉNÉRAL DE GAULLE, 1050 IXELLES

Architect: René Ajoux

Built: 1939

Avenue de la Cascade, after which this building is named, and which extends along the Ixelles ponds, was renamed avenue Général De Gaulle after World War II in the French president's honour. Its ocean liner design and its cladding with white ceramics had led to this building sometimes being called *the bathroom of Ixelles*. There is a wave-like feel to the design, in the combination of the façade's volumes and the gate of the front garden, in the corner windows and the ceilings of the terraces. The rounded entrance is framed by two porthole-shaped windows.

◀ La Cascade

APARTMENT BUILDINGS

After World War I, the construction of apartment buildings for the middle class boomed in Brussels, for practical and financial reasons and following the implementation of the Law of 8 July 1924, which made the principle of co-ownership legal. Until then, this type of dwelling was never a success with the affluent classes, who preferred a lifestyle based on private dwellings. The Société Belge Immobilière (SBI), which was founded in 1922, was the first company to take advantage of this change in legislation and promote this type of housing to the middle class. The apartments it built were originally inspired by the Beaux-Arts style, in an attempt to convince its hesitant clientele. From 1925, the buildings were more original, more modern. Other real estate companies also started to build apartment buildings, for rent or for sale. They include Jean-Florian Collin's Études et Réalisations immobilières (ETRIMO) and Compagnie générale d'Entreprise immobilière (COGENI). These companies resorted to rational and modern building techniques, used reinforced concrete for the structure and foundations of these apartment buildings. These buildings offered all the comfort of the old town houses on several floors, but one single floor, with the added plus of mod cons, such as lifts, fitted kitchens, bathrooms, a concierge, garages, a garbage chute, central heating, a laundry room, wall cupboards, a telephone...

The apartments were subdivided into three autonomous zones, which corresponded to the division in several floors of the old town houses, which were separated from each other with hallways and corridors: the reception rooms, the private rooms (bedrooms, bathrooms) and rooms for domestic purposes (kitchen, study, maid's room). The reception rooms received special attention and were often vast and on the façade side. The shared spaces of these buildings were also very luxurious, revealing the occupants' social status to visitors. The Residence Palace holds a special place in the history of apartment buildings in Brussels. The CEO of Crédit général hypothécaire, Lucien Kaisin, tasked the Swiss-born architect Michel Polak (1885-1948) with the design of the huge Residence Palace (1922-1927), which combined all the assets of a luxury hotel and the city for millionaires. The building, in rue de la Loi, had 180 apartments, with 8 to 22 rooms, and a host of exceptional services: a theatre, restaurants that delivered food to your home with a dumbwaiter, a pool, a fencing hall and a gym, tennis courts, a garage, a shop, a bank, a post office... A cosmopolitan elite moved in, thereby giving its seal of approval to this new housing concept and convincing the middle class. The building, which was commandeered by the Germans in 1941, was acquired by the Belgian State in 1947, which converted it into an administrative building.

5/ RÉSIDENCE BELLE-VUE

50, AVENUE GÉNÉRAL DE GAULLE, 1050 IXELLES

Architect: Stanislas Jasinski
Built: 1933

Stanislas Jasinski (1901-1978) trained with several architects in Brussels and Paris, including Henry van de Velde. He was regularly asked to build apartments buildings for real estate companies, creating some of Brussels' most beautiful apartment buildings, with a pure and elegant design. He also built houses, villas, designed interiors and helped build hospitals. On the outside, this corner building, which he designed for ETRIMO, and which is clad with white stone, has a rounded entrance, surmounted with a cylindrical projection running the length of the building. The span with porthole-shaped windows is reminiscent of an ocean liner. At the time, writers extolled the qualities of this building, its location, its layout and its beautiful finish.[1] The building, which is proportionate to the open space in front of it, had a lovely view of the ponds. Authors were unhappy about the many apartment buildings with multiple floors that were being built in secondary, narrow streets. There was an apartment on every floor of this building, with a floor area of 200 m^2, divided into three separate zones: the living and its rotunda in the centre, which was separated from the dining room with terrace by a wide glass window, with the study, the kitchen and two maid's rooms at the rear. To the right of the entrance, a separate hall led to four bedrooms and two bathrooms for the apartment's owners. So there was a clear division between the reception rooms, the private rooms of the owners and the realm of the domestic help. The structure of this building, made entirely out of reinforced concrete, meant that the architect did not have to stick to this fixed layout and was able to alter the spaces.

▼ Résidence Belle-Vue

▼ Floor plan of the 5th floor. Taken from La Technique des Travaux, No. 3, 1937, p. 117

6/ LE TONNEAU

51, AVENUE GÉNÉRAL DE GAULLE, 1050 IXELLES

Architect: Jean-Florian Collin, with Stanislas Jasinski
Built: 1939-1940
Listed: 19/4/2007

This apartment building, which clearly has some similarities with the design of an ocean liner and which is clad with pink cement, lives up to its name. Its ribbon windows are interrupted by a central, glazed span, capped with vertical spurs, which are so typical of Collin's work. Jean-Florian Collin (1904-1985), a self-made man, architect, real estate developer and liberal politician, set up a business as an architect-builder in 1926. After declaring bankruptcy for the first time in 1932, he established ETRIMO (Études et Réalisations immobilières) in 1935, becoming a spearhead for modernist middle-class apartment buildings. After the war, ETRIMO specialised in the construction of medium-sized housing, which no longer had the same architectural quality or attention to urban integration, which was so typical of the buildings of the Thirties. Collin declared bankruptcy again in 1970.

Let's continue our walk to avenue Émile Duray. This avenue, which extends along La Cambre Abbay, was built for the World Expo of 1910 at Solbosch. The buildings along it all date from the interwar period and include several Art Deco-inspired town houses: No. 4: 1928, Fernand Petit; No. 6: 1924, arch. Adrien Blomme; No. 12: 1925, arch. Michel Polak; No. 14: 1925, arch. Fernand Petit; No. 18 and No. 20, 1924, arch. Adrien Blomme.

◄ Le Tonneau

▼ Avenue Duray in Ixelles

LA CAMBRE, AN ARCHITECTURAL SCHOOL

The site of the former La Cambre Abbey is now home to the renowned architecture and visuals arts school with the same name. In the early twentieth century, Belgium had various architectural programmes, with different approaches: artistic in the academies, technical/scientific in the engineering and artisanal schools of the Écoles Saint-Luc. In 1926, the La Cambre Decorative Arts School was founded. The first academic year started in 1927. Under the impetus of its founder and first director, Henry van de Velde, La Cambre became synonymous with an extremely original approach to the arts, with students learning the different styles, in the same vein as the Bauhaus School in Germany. La Cambre added modern, contemporary architecture to its programme and attracted several modernist architects as lecturers including Jean-Jules Eggericx, Louis Herman De Koninck, Victor Bourgeois, Antoine Pompe...

7/ GROUP OF DWELLINGS

1-27, SQUARE DU VAL DE LA CAMBRE, 1050 IXELLES

Architect: Adrien Blomme
Built: 1925-1932

The Compagnie générale d'Entreprise immobilière (COGENI) tasked Adrien Blomme with the job of designing a plan for this close, with a main entrance along avenue Duray. Originally a private road, this subdivision shows how the wealthy classes wanted to isolate themselves from the city. At the same time, it was apparent, at the time, that these small urban islands had to be densely built up, for financial reasons but also because space was becoming an increasingly rare commodity. This subdivision is built around a square and extends, beyond the covered entrance with its pinnacle, to avenue de l'Hippodrome, with various winding roads. For the most part, it is made up of private homes, and one large apartment building.
Adrien Blomme built or designed the plans for most of the houses, which were inspired by medieval and Baroque architecture. The square's ambience is similar to that of a beguinage or a garden city.

At 52, avenue Émile Duray, a modernist house that was built by COGENI was recently restored (arch. Charles Bartels, 1928).

At No. 58, avenue Duray, the corner building by Adrien Blomme, also for COGENI, is very different in style from the rest of square Val de la Cambre. This was the first apartment building by the architect, and was built on a corner parcel at that. Blomme liked this kind of challenge, as this allowed him to create original plans and sweeping views. There are two apartments on every floor, and they are particularly spacious (more than 300 m²). Originally, they had two bathrooms for three bedrooms, vast reception spaces and service spaces, with a separate lift. The finish was equally detailed: mosaic, parquet and tile floors, mouldings, wood panelling, metal frames, wall cupboards...

▾▸ Square du Val de la Cambre

ADRIEN BLOMME (1878-1940)

The talented and prolific architect Adrien Blomme built many buildings in Brussels, for a wealthy clientele, comprising urban developments, apartment buildings and villas in styles that range from Art Nouveau to Art Deco and even neo-Baroque. Promoting the continuity between tradition and the innovations of his era, Blomme believed an architectural work was a gesamtkunstwerk, including all the disciplines, from urban planning to interior design and even landscaping. Blomme stood out on the architectural landscape of the interwar period. Approaching every project as a specific case for a different client, he adapted his style to the needs and wishes of his clients. His first designs, from 1906-1907, combined a certain traditionalism in design with Art Nouveau. After World War I, he participated in the reconstruction of the country, undertaking several large building projects for COGENI. Subsequently the Wielemans family (of the eponymous brewery) became his patrons. He built an Art Deco town house for them in Brussels, with a patio that is entirely clad with azulejos (14, rue Defacqz, 1928), a monumental brewing hall for the factories in Forest (1930), Cinema Métropole (30, rue Neuve, 1932), he expanded the Metropole Hotel and the Aux Armes des Brasseurs café (56-58, bd Anspach, 1939-1941). He had a large family and in the early Thirties, he decided to collaborate with his son Yvan (19061961) with whom he built apartment buildings and Gare du Midi in Brussels (with F. Petit, 1938-1950, demolished). Adrien Blomme died in the early days of May 1940, in the Red Cross Clinic in Ixelles, following gallbladder surgery, experiencing deep anguish over the fact that he had no news from his three sons who had all been called to arms.

8/ PALAIS DE LA CAMBRE

60-68, AVENUE ÉMILE DURAY, 4, AVENUE DE LA FOLLE CHANSON, 1050 IXELLES AND BRUSSELS

Architect: Camille Damman
Built: 1924

Built on the site of a former velodrome, of which you can still see the reinforced concrete structure in the cellars, Palais de La Cambre is actually a monumental group of five apartment buildings. The overview is slightly hampered these days by the fact that the façades were not all cleaned at the same time, drawing attention to the divisions between the buildings. This Art Deco building was built for the SBI and presented as a scale model at the International Exhibition of Modern Decorative and Industrial Arts in Paris in 1925. The most interesting place to look at this ensemble is opposite 64-66, avenue Duray. These two apartment buildings feature a line of monumental sculptures and bas-relief friezes. The spiralled motifs of the ironwork on the garden fences is replicated in the balcony railings.

The monumental entrances are surmounted by sculptured bas-reliefs and the inner faces are decorated with stylised heads, which resemble antique masques.

▸ Palais de la Cambre, entrance, 4, av. de la Folle Chanson

9/ PALAIS DE LA FOLLE CHANSON

2, BOULEVARD GÉNÉRAL JACQUES, 1050 IXELLES

Architect: Antoine Courtens
Built: 1928
Listed: 8/8/1988 and 25/10/2001

The name of this apartment building, with apartments for sale, refers to the eponymous statue by Jef Lambeaux, which originally stood not far from here. This eight-floor building stands out because of its corner rotunda, which is underscored by a monumental blue stone entrance, surmounted by a campanile with a cupola. Antoine Courtens (1899-1969) is regarded as one of the main representatives of the Art Deco movement in Brussels. Born into a family of artists, he had the opportunity to pursue his architectural training during many trips and work placements with famous architects in France and Germany. He also worked for Victor Horta, contributing to the design of the Centre for Fine Arts. From 1926 onwards, he received several important commissions, like the Palais de la Folle Chanson or the Haerens house (av. Brugmann in Uccle, 1928). They are considered to be among the most accomplished examples of Art Deco buildings in Brussels, combining Horta's influence with that of the Parisian designers with whom he worked. Courtens often also designed the interiors for his projects, including the furniture, the luminaires and the rugs. Ironwork became one of his specialities. At the end of the Thirties, he evolved towards a more attenuated modernist style, which is especially apparent in his design for the Domaine de l'Estérel (1936-1938), a large sport and residential building in Les Laurentides, in Québec, which he built for Louis Empain.

The programme of the Palais de la Folle Chanson is rather complex and was clearly designed to fulfil the requirements of a wealthy clientele, with cellars, garages, a concierge apartment, a monumental stairwell, four lifts including two for domestic help, two apartments on every floor, large reception rooms, maid's rooms, terraces and so on. The entrance and the hallway behind it are elegantly decorated with different types of marble, including gilded travertine, brushed glass lamps, ironwork with Art Deco motifs, steel radiator covers... The eighth floor, which was solely for servants, is set back. Two large terraces were built on either side of the star-shaped turret, for the co-owners. The space under the cupola was also a common area and could be used as a reading or smoking room. Originally, the façades were covered with a new type of material, washed granito, which mimicked Euville stone and was produced using crushed marble and cement that was coloured with mineral pigments. As the coating deteriorated over time, it was replaced with a new finish in the original colour during the restoration.

◀ Palais de la Folle Chanson, entrance hall

Palais de la Folle Chanson ▶

10/ RÉSIDENCE ERNESTINE

3, ROND-POINT DE L'ÉTOILE, 1050 IXELLES

Architect: Jean-Florian Collin
Built: 1939

Nowadays, the congested rond-point de l'Étoile has very few appealing features. In the Twenties and Thirties, things must have been quite different given that several prestigious apartment buildings were built here. The corners of these buildings are rounded, with plenty of windows. The living rooms are located in this span, and enjoy sweeping views and have plenty of light. Résidence Ernestine, an ETRIMO building, in the ocean liner style, is no different. The façade is a typical Collin composition, with rows of horizontal windows that are intersected with vertical spans. There were three apartments on every floor, including one large one with ten rooms, including a salon, a dining room and a smoking room in the corner span.

Jean-Florian Collin also built the Palais du Congo (1930) apartment building at 2, avenue du Congo (to the right of the previous building), in a more traditional Art Deco style.

On the opposite side of the street, at 20, boulevard Général Jacques, the Résidence de la Cambre (1936), Brussels' first skyscraper, was the outcome of a collaboration between the architect Marcel Peeters and an investor called Gérard Kaisin.

The apartment building at 23, avenue Jeanne (1933) is an excellent example of the rather classical output of Jacques Saintenoy (1895-1947), an architect who built several luxurious apartment buildings near avenue Louise and the Ixelles ponds. The building has a lively façace with protruding rounded balconies, and an elegant finish. There was an apartment on every floor. The reception rooms were on the street side. Saintenoy himself lived there and also build the house next door, at No. 25 (1933).

On the opposite side of the street, at No. 52, a private house, built by Fernand Petit (1930), is now home to the offices of the Université libre de Bruxelles.

We now walk to avenue Franklin D. Roosevelt, which was originally called avenue des Nations. This avenue, which was built in 1920 on the site of the World Expo of 1910, soon attracted the upper classes, who built prestigious town houses, villas and apartment buildings here. On the uneven side, the City of Brussels required that vast gaps be left between the buildings to ensure La Cambre Forest remained visible. A series of large villas in different styles of the Twenties and Thirties were built here, including Beaux-Arts, Art Deco... On the even side, beyond the campus, the buildings are joined and built on narrower parcels.

◂ Résidence Ernestine

11/ DOUBLE HÔTEL DE BODT

27-29, AVENUE FRANKLIN ROOSEVELT, 1050 BRUSSELS

Architect: Henry van de Velde
Built: 1931-1932
Listed: 16/3/1995

This double, modernist town house was built for father and son De Bodt. From the outside it looks like one and the same large villa, as the entrances to the two houses were integrated on different sides. The villa is situated on a slightly inclined rectangular parcel of land, and has a shared garden. The various service spaces are located in the cellar (the house on the right also had a gym, which gave out directly onto the garden, opposite a rectangular water basin). The reception rooms were on the ground floor, the bedrooms and private apartments on the upper floors. Initially, the façade was supposed to be built in white stone, but the architect requested a derogation, asking to use Belvédère brick instead, which was cheaper and used more frequently. *These rough, large bricks resemble Spanish bricks, with horizontal, recessed joints. Van de Velde required a special shape and a special firing for the rounded corners.*[2] The interiors have since been renovated, without having an impact on the house's exterior. Hôtel de Bodt now belongs to the Wallonia-Brussels Federation and is used by ENSAV La Cambre. It is currently being restored.

◀ Hôtel De Bodt

On the opposite side, at 50, avenue Roosevelt, Building A of the Université libre de Bruxelles, which was built in 1924-1928, stands out because of its belfry tower. The university was forced to leave the city centre in the Twenties, moving to this land, which it received from the City of Brussels, along avenue des Nations. The building was built for the Faculties of Philosophy, Arts and Law, the administration and the library. Its Flemish neo-Renaissance style, of national inspiration, was imposed by the Commission for Relief in Belgium Educational Foundation, an American organisation which promoted university studies in Belgium after World War I, and which funded the building. Its architect Alexis Dumont built several other rather modernist buildings.

At No. 39-41, two twin villas in a very simple Art Deco style were built in 1928-1930 by Adrien Blomme for traders who worked in the city centre. Today it is occupied by the ULB's Institute for European Studies. No. 39 was the residence of Elie Benezra, who sold Iranian oriental carpets, for whom Blomme also built a shop in rue de l'Ecuyer. The decorative motifs on this villa are clearly inspired by Mediterranean designs and include spiral columns near the corner windows. The façade at No. 41 has five semi-circular arched windows.

▾ Building A of the Université libre de Bruxelles, av. Roosevelt 50, arch. A. Dumont

12/ PRIVATE HOME AND APARTMENT BUILDING

52, AVENUE FRANKLIN ROOSEVELT AND 1, AVENUE ANTOINE DEPAGE, 1050 BRUSSELS

Architect: Adrien Blomme

Built: 1928

In 1927, Adrien Blomme acquired some land in a public sale, which gave him the opportunity to build his third home. He elaborated the following programme: *to build a building for an architect aged 50, who was married and a father of six, with two daughters and four sons.*[3] To save money, he also added *three small apartments and two larger ones, for tenants, which were separate from his home and office.*[4]

Blomme submitted a simple design, without superfluous decoration, to the City of Brussels, for economic reasons and also because of personal preferences. These plans were rejected for reasons of aesthetics and size. The architect then sent his project to his colleagues, asking them to comment on it, and then submitted it again to the city, without making any changes. He did, however, add a series of letters of support.

◀ Former home and office of Adrien Blomme

These include letters from Victor Horta, Alexis Dumont, Fernand Petit and a letter from Société belge des Urbanistes et Architectes modernistes (SBUAM).[5] They all unanimously recognised the quality of the project. Petit even rejoiced in the fact that his friend abandoned his marked preference for picturesque charm of recent years. The SBUAM's letter argued in favour of a modern architecture, as opposed to pastiche architecture, and criticised the new buildings of the ULB, calling them *lamentable anachronisms and examples of the grotesque, considering them an abomination along these new arteries that run into the city.* These letters are a summary of all the traditional arguments between proponents of the old and the new style, and avenue des Nations regularly was on the receiving end. This diversity of styles, which today is one of the points of interest of this avenue, elicited several acrimonious debates and sharp criticism in its day.

Blomme respected the planning rules of the neighbourhood, building three floors on the side of avenue des Nations and five floors along avenue Depage. He then designed a cylinder that connected the two wings with their different levels, to achieve a more harmonious appearance. The building's structure is mixed, with reinforced concrete and load-bearing masonry. It was coated with a light-coloured coating. The building has three entrances, which are also indicative of the building's former layout: 1. Main entrance of Blomme's house, on the corner, with two bas-reliefs by Ossip Zadkino, featuring the architect's attributes, i.e., the square, the tee, the compass, the scale model... The entrance led into a vast rounded hall with a staircase to the first floor. The living room with three semi-circular arched windows was situated on the corner of the first floor and gave out onto a terrace. The dining room and architect's study were also on this floor. The bedrooms and a breakfast room were on the second floor. A large drawing studio occupied the third floor. 2. The servant's entrance and garage were in avenue des Nations. A staircase connected the service spaces on the ground floor with the upper floors. 3. The entrance in avenue Depage led to the rented apartments and the drawing studio. After Ms Blomme died, the ULB acquired the building to use it as the rector's offices. The hallways and certain walls were altered, but the panelling, parquet and marble floors maintained, attesting to the house's former splendour. Since the rector moved to new premises, the building is now home to an institute of the ULB.

At 5, avenue Depage, a modernist house (arch. Walthère Michel, 1928-1930) features a series of oriental motifs on the façade. Chinese tiles were used to cover the roof of the projecting part of the house. At the time of its construction, the client lived in Hong Kong.

The Cohen house at No. 60 avenue Roosevelt was built in 1927 by Henry van de Velde, with Stanislas Jasinski. This modernist house features a pared down, monumental design, with a symmetrical stone façade, with three spans, with windows that are flush with the masonry. Van de Velde designed the house, the interior and its furniture for a factory owner called Georges Cohen. He also subsequently built him a factory in Ninove. The Austrian government acquired the building in 1968. It is currently used as a residence by the Austrian ambassador to Belgium.

▾ Former home and office of Adrien Blomme, plan of the first floor. Taken from La Technique des Travaux, No. 8, 1931, p. 472

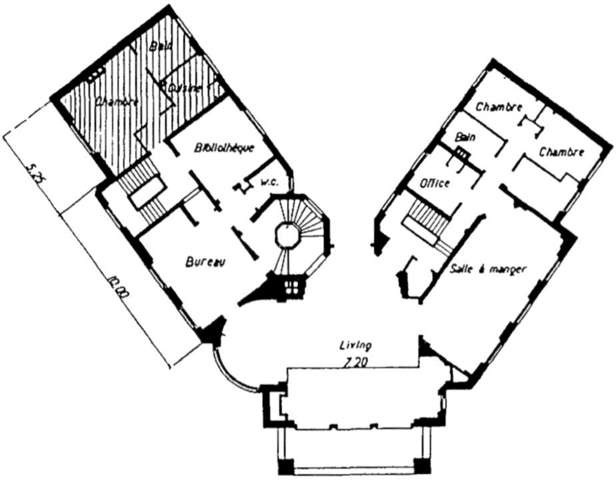

A brief detour through the Solbosch neighbourhood is an excellent opportunity to discover a series of buildings:

- On the corner of avenue Roosevelt and avenue de l'Orée, a group of buildings, consisting of a private home (78, av. Roosevelt and 5, av. de l'Orée) and two modernist homes (7-9, av. de l'Orée) was built in 1934 by the architects R. Théry and J. de Wit van der Hoop for Jules Hoste (1884-1954), a liberal politician, a figurehead of the Flemish movement, who succeeded his father as director of the newspaper *Het Laatste Nieuws*. The recently restored town house is now occupied by the Embassy of Niger.
- Two apartment buildings at 19-21, avenue de l'Orée (arch. Jean-Florian Collin, 1935).
- Résidence Orée at 23, avenue de l'Orée, (arch. Stanislas Jasinski, 1936). This bright sunny modernist apartment building attracted wealthy occupants for whom the architect also designed several interiors.
- An apartment building at 6, square du Solbosch, on the corner of av. Guillaume Gilbert, (arch. Alexis Dumont and Marcel Van Goethem, 1935) in which the architects combined protruding balconies to emphasise the angle of the building.
- A small apartment building at 29, square du Solbosch (arch. JeanJules Eggericx, 1925) whose window frames and the use of dark brick are reminiscent of the Wolfers-Petrucci house (18, rue De Praetere in Ixelles, 1925), and the buildings of the Dutch De Stijl movement. Jean-Jules Eggericx (1884-1963) became famous for his investment in garden-cities (Le Logis and Floréal, Watermael-Boitsfort) as well as the private dwellings and apartment buildings he built, including the twin Léopold and Albert residences in square de Meeus (1935-1940).
- In avenue Général Dossin de Saint-Georges, St Adrian's Church (arch. Auguste Vanden Nieuwenborg, 1938) stands out because of its monumental design, with a tall tower, which has been integrated in the façade. The façade has decorative brickwork around the openings, like the portal. The interior is also very refined.
- Two apartment buildings at 32 (1936-1937) and 34 (1934), avenue des Phalènes (arch. JeanFlorian Collin).
- A modernist house at 27, avenue des Phalènes (arch. Léon E. Govaerts and Alexis Van Vaerenbergh, 1934).
- An Art Deco investment property at 5, avenue des Phalènes 5, (arch. J.-B. Van Den Broeck, 1933) with an entrance in the shape of a parabolic arch, which is surmounted by a transom window with a geometric stained-glass window.

▸ Entrance of the apartment building at 5, av. des Phalènes, arch. J.-B. Van Den Broeck

13/ PRIVATE HOME

90, AVENUE FRANKLIN ROOSEVELT, 1050 BRUSSELS

Architect: Georges Dedoyard
Built: 1930

The owner of this house, who originally hailed from Liège, tasked a Liège-based architect with the design of his home in Brussels. While Georges Dedoyard (1897-1988) stuck to the Art Deco style for this design, he evolved towards a more modernist style over time. This corner building features an original composition and refined decoration. It was recently restored. The Euville stone façade is decorated with bas-reliefs (including a panel representing a sunset, over the entrance), with ironwork with fountain motifs and iridescent ceramics. The original design included a bronze sculpture representing a man, at the top of the building, on the corner. The interior layout of this simple and spacious house included an office/study on the ground floor in the corner. The dining room was situated to the right of the entrance and gave out onto a terrace. The upper floors, with a lift, comprised several sitting rooms, bathrooms and bedrooms. The roof was transformed into a terrace to make up for the lack of a garden.

▼ Private home, 90, avenue Roosevelt

An Art Nouveau villa at 86, avenue Roosevelt, which was built before the World Expo of 1910 (arch. Léon Delune, 1906).

At No. 98, an embassy now occupies this house by Adrien Blomme (1930).

At No. 106, this tiny Art Deco gem was built in 1930 for a businessman called Jules Van Oncem. The symmetry and the various protruding segments and geometric mouldings are its distinguishing characteristics. The door on the left led to Van Oncem's offices, at the rear, while the door on the right served as the entrance to his home, on the upper floors. The adjoining building (108) was built in 1931 by the same businessman.

14/ VILLA EMPAIN / BOGHOSSIAN FOUNDATION

67, AVENUE FRANKLIN ROOSEVELT AND 32, AVENUE VICTORIA, 1050 BRUSSELS

Architect: Polak Michel, with Alfred Hoch
Built: 1930-1934
Listed: 29/3/2007

Louis Empain was just twenty years old when he asked Michel Polak, the architect of the Résidence Palace and several other prestigious buildings in the city centre, to build this villa for him. He was the younger son of Baron Edouard Empain, an industrialist and investor, who had made his fortune building railways and underground lines. Louis Empain (1908-1976) was a philanthropist and patron of the arts. In the Thirties, he asked Antoine Courtens to build him a recreational area in Canada. This property consists of a monumental villa with four façades, as well as a garden. The main feature of the garden is the pool, which is surrounded by a pergola, and pilasters, on the side of avenue Victoria. It is surrounded by a blue stone enclosure, with wrought iron railings with geometric patterns. The villa's overall appearance is very classic and refined and you can clearly feel the influence of the Stoclet Palace here. But it also has a modernist feel, because of the construction techniques the architect used, and the clear layout of the building. The façade in polished grey granite from Baveno is very simple. The volumes of the building and the window frames are accentuated with bronzed brass angles, which have been re-gilded. The double entrance door, with wrought iron elements with abstract patterns, is surmounted by an awning that is visually supported by

▾ Villa Empain / Boghossian Foundation, main façade

luminous sconces on the consoles. This is also the only decorative element of this façade. The interior spaces are arranged around a large central hall, on two levels, with a large skylight through which the light falls in. The offices were situated on the ground floor, on the side of the avenue, whereas the reception rooms were at the rear of the house, extending out to the terrace and the pool. An intimate sitting room and bar had a staircase that led directly to the upper floor and the owner's bedroom. The various rooms could be accessed from the gallery. Originally the plans included a study or an arms room on the street side. The servant's rooms were situated on the second floor and were slightly set back. The sun terrace for the owners was on the garden side. The kitchen and service spaces, as well as the vault, were in the cellar. The elegant interior design, with luxurious materials, was finely executed using various types of marble and wood, with wrought iron railings and grates with geometric motifs, which are attributed to the Brussels craftsman Alfred François and the Frenchman Edgard Brandt, as well as bronze elements, gilded engraved glass and so on.

Louis Empain briefly lived here. In 1937, he donated the villa to the Belgian state, to be used as a Decorative Arts Museum. During the war years, the Germans commandeered the building. In 1945, it was rented to the Russian embassy. This annoyed Louis Empain, who undertook steps to have his property returned to him in 1964. He then hosted cultural events there. In 1973, the villa was sold, and rented out for ten years to the TV channel RTL. In the Nineties, it was rarely occupied and then sold again. It soon started to deteriorate, leading to unfortunate renovations. In 2007, the villa was listed and acquired by the Boghossian Foundation, which entrusted its restoration to Francis Metzger of Ma2 architecture. It reopened to the public in the spring of 2010, as an arts centre, promoting exchanges between the cultures of the east and west.

▾ Villa Empain / Boghossian Foundation, gallery on the first floor and skylight

▾ Villa Empain / Boghossian Foundation, plan of the ground floor. Taken from La Technique des Travaux, No. 8, 1935, p. 397

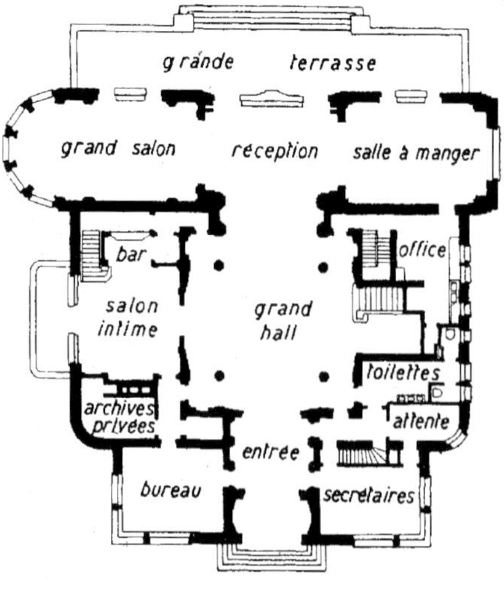

15/ APARTMENT BUILDING

4, AVENUE DES SCARABÉES, 1050 BRUSSELS

Architect: Stanislas Jasinski
Built: 1933

The façade of this modernist building combines convex and concave elements, which point to its interior layout as a duplex. It consists of three apartments and was designed to offer its occupants all the advantages of a private home on a relatively narrow strip of land. The lower floor of each apartment is occupied by a smoking room or study and a vast living room at the front. The dining room and kitchen are situated at the rear. In the centre of the apartment, the vast hall opens out on two floors, with a staircase leading to the bedrooms. While this hall is rather dark and occupies a lot of space, it also permanently connected the floors, while separating the daytime spaces from the night-time spaces. This duplex layout is rather rare in Brussels apartment buildings from this era. However, it was often used in modernist dwellings.

At 22, avenue des Scarabées, the apartment building of Jean-Florian Collin (1932-1934) is easy to recognise with its vertical central span, with windows. There are two apartments on every floor. Most of the original metal window frames were replaced.

At No. 9, an investment property (arch. Francis J. Meunier, 1938) with a white stone façade and a blue stone base stands out because of its wrought iron door, with geometric motifs, surmounted by a stone bas-relief featuring a scarab.

Now let's walk back to avenue Roosevelt and stop at No. 114 (arch. Maurice Uyttenhoven, 1935). This modernist house has been remarkably well preserved.

▾ Apartment building, 4, av. des Scarabées

At No. 116, avenue Roosevelt, you will run into an Art Deco building (arch. Joe Ramaekers and Robert Michiels, 1935) with a façade that is perfectly divided in two, by the central axis that starts from the entrance. While the design is rather simple, the combination of protruding rounded lateral balconies, with geometric ironwork, adds a nice flourish.

The modernist house at No. 180, with its white coated façade and base of yellow Belvédère bricks is one of the rare houses along this avenue to be signed by A. et Y. Blomme associés (1935).

The investment property at No. 186 (arch. J.-B. Van Den Broeck, 1936), with its reconstituted stone façade, is decorated with lavish and elaborate geometric shapes. The entrance, with two porthole-shaped windows on either side, also features original decorative motifs.

◄ Apartment building, 116, av. Roosevelt, arch. J. Ramaekers and R. Michiels

▼ Apartment building, 186, av. Roosevelt, arch. J.-B. Van Den Broeck

16/ VILLA

3, AVENUE DU BRÉSIL, 1050 BRUSSELS

Architect: Raphaël Delville
Built: 1937

This modernist villa occupies the entire width of this parcel. The garage is in a small separate building, at the rear, and connects with the villa with a concrete pergola. Originally, the quartz slabs that were used to clad the façade were pinkish in colour, and therefore less bright in the sunlight. The reinforced concrete villa has an open-plan layout. The reception rooms, the kitchen and an office for a liberal profession, with a separate entrance, were all located on the ground floor while the bedrooms were on the first floor. Delville, who was also a painter and a sculptor, liked to incorporate artwork in his façades. Originally, he intended to add a bas-relief above the entrance, but following a misunderstanding, the owner selected a classic artwork, from the mouldings department of the Cinquantenaire Museum instead. The architect also designed the villa's interior. Part of the interior has been preserved in spite of the fact that it is now occupied by offices.

Villa, av. du Brésil 3 ▸

P
A SUIVRE ....

SECOND WALK

ART DECO ALONG THE CANAL

SAILLANT DE L'YSER TO L'ARCHIDUC

During this walk, you can discover a more commercial neighbourhood of Brussels' Pentagon, which was already thriving during the 1930s, with the warehouses of the maritime quarter, the trendy shops in rue Dansaert today, the Citroën garage... There are also plenty of residential buildings, including apartment buildings for the most part, which catered to the lower and middle classes. Finally, this neighbourhood was also a nightlife district, with the famous Art Deco piano bar L'Archiduc, among others. During this walk you'll see plenty of references to the Great War, in the names of the streets and the buildings, including Saillant de l'Yser, boulevard d'Ypres and de Dixmude, rue de la Forêt d'Houthulst... The authorities and the real estate developers of the interwar period paid tribute to recent events in the toponymy.

◂ Apartment buildings, 85-101, rue A. Dansaert, arch. L. Duhayon and M. Julien

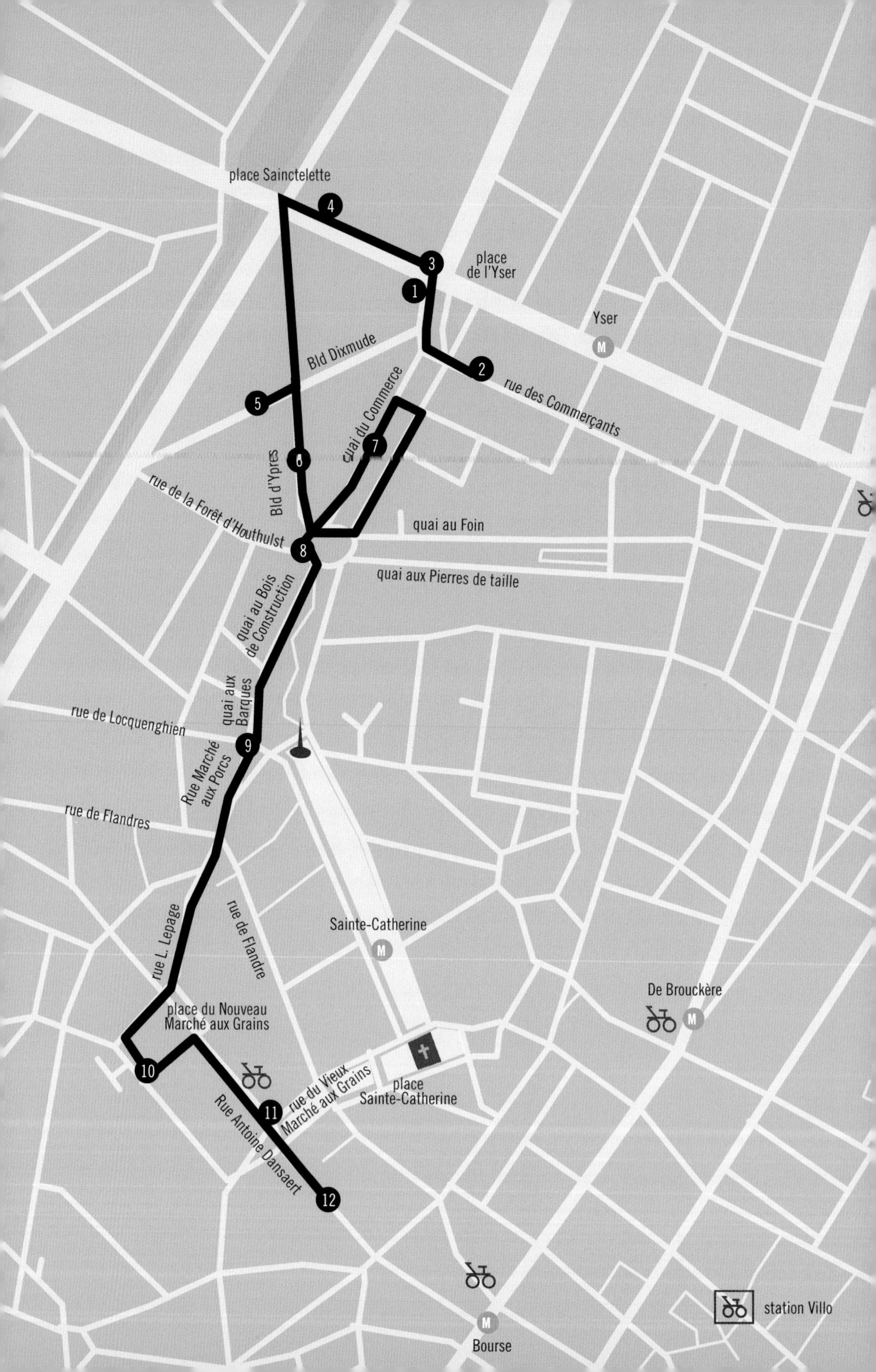

place Sainctelette
place de l'Yser
Yser
Bld Dixmude
quai du Commerce
rue des Commerçants
Bld d'Ypres
rue de la Forêt d'Houthulst
quai au Foin
quai aux Pierres de taille
quai au Bois de Construction
quai aux Barques
rue de Locquenghien
Rue Marché aux Porcs
rue de Flandres
rue de Flandre
rue L. Lepage
Sainte-Catherine
De Brouckère
place du Nouveau Marché aux Grains
rue du Vieux Marché aux Grains
place Sainte-Catherine
Rue Antoine Dansaert
Bourse
station Villo

01 LE SAILLANT DE L'YSER
6, place de l'Yser, 32-40, boulevard de Dixmude and 1-9, square Sainctelette, 1000 Brussels

02 ANCIENS ÉTABLISSEMENTS BLUM / BLUM HABERDASHERY
67, rue des Commerçants, 1000 Brussels

03 ANCIENS ÉTABLISSEMENTS CITROËN / CITROËN GARAGE
7, place de l'Yser, 1000 Brussels

04 KAAITHEATER
20, place Sainctelette and 4, quai des Péniches, 1000 Brussels

05 HALLES AMERICA
21-29, boulevard de Dixmude, 1000 Brussels

06 RETAIL AND APARTMENT BUILDING
34-36, boulevard d'Ypres, 1000 Brussels

07 APARTMENT BUILDING
20-22, quai du Commerce, 1000 Brussels

08 FORÊT D'HOUTHULST SOCIAL HOUSING PROJECT
2-12, boulevard d'Ypres and 1-17, rue de la Forêt d'Houthulst, 1000 Brussels

09 APARTMENT BUILDING
10-32, rue du Marché aux Porcs and 2, rue Locquenghien, 1000 Brussels

10 FORMER WAREHOUSE
22-23, place du Nouveau Marché aux Grains, 1000 Brussels

11 RETAIL AND APARTMENT BUILDING
75-79, rue Antoine Dansaert and 7-11, rue du Vieux Marché aux Grains, 1000 Brussels

12 L'ARCHIDUC
6, rue Antoine Dansaert, 1000 Brussels

1/ LE SAILLANT DE L'YSER

6, PLACE DE L'YSER, 32-40, BOULEVARD DE DIXMUDE AND 1-9, SQUARE SAINCTELETTE, 1000 BRUSSELS

Architects: Louis Duhayon and Marcel Julien
Built: 1925, 1926 and 1930

This elegant Art Deco building is a beacon and landmark at the top of the wide avenues that were built for the World Exhibition on the Heysel in 1935. The Parisian architects Duhayon and Julien, who collaborated for several years, built several buildings in Brussels for the Société belge immobilière (SBI). They also built several private homes, buildings and mansions in Paris and the surrounding region, including the Royal Monceau.

The distinctive corner wedge of the building, with its 11 floors and dome, is tucked in between two smaller wings. The façades, which have been clad in faux white stone, on a marble base, are decorated with Art Deco motifs and feature bow windows and balconies that extend along the building, emphasising the horizontal design of some of the floors...

▼ Le Saillant de l'Yser

2/ ANCIENS ÉTABLISSEMENTS BLUM / BLUM HABERDASHERY

67, RUE DES COMMERÇANTS, 1000 BRUSSELS

Architect: Fernand Conard – Built: 1933
Listed: 12/3/1998

In 1933, Établissements Blum, which specialised in haberdashery, decided to build a warehouse in rue des Commerçants, tacking it onto the back of a late nineteenth-century mansion in boulevard d'Anvers. The offices and reception rooms were installed in a preserved section of the former mansion, whereas the warehouse itself was built in a more functionalist style.

The façade, which was completed in 1934, according to the date on the pediment, is stripped of any ornamentation. It has three central spans, with windows that extend across all three floors. These accentuate the vertical design and draw daylight into the vast hall, on which three superimposed galleries open out, under a large concrete and glass tiled dome. In 1998, the advertising agency Duval Guillaume moved into the building, entrusting the architect Jo Crepain with its renovation.

◀ Anciens Établissements Blum

3/ ANCIENS ÉTABLISSEMENTS CITROËN / CITROËN GARAGE

7, PLACE DE L'YSER, 1000 BRUSSELS

Architects: Alexis Dumont and Marcel Van Goethem – Built: 1933-1934

In the early Thirties, the Citroën car brand, which was growing at a rapid pace by then, acquired a plot of land, which was situated just 500 metres from gare du Nord/North Station. Here it built one of the largest garages and sales rooms in Europe, with an American-style showroom. The architects Dumont and Van Goethem were tasked with the design of this gigantic two-part steel and glass building, working with Maurice Ravazé, the Citroën company's head architect. The large showroom with its 25-metre high, curved façade dominates place de l'Yser and originally only consisted of a ground floor, with a large glass window.

In 1959, the showroom was subdivided into the different floors that are still there today. The garage itself was built along quai de Willebroeck, quai de la Voirie and quai des Péniches, and gave out onto the showroom. The vast space, measuring 130 x 102 metres, comprised a petrol station, the workshops, the parts warehouse and the offices. This monumental functionalist building with its aerodynamic shape embodied the avant-garde techniques Citroën used. The building is now owned by the Brussels-Capital Region and is now operated by KANAL-Centre Pompidou. In 2022, it will open as a new modern, contemporary and architecture museum, sharing the premises with CIVA, the Centre d'Architecture bruxellois.

◀ Anciens établissements Citroën

4/ KAAITHEATER

20, PLACE SAINCTELETTE AND 4, QUAI DES PÉNICHES, 1000 BRUSSELS

Architect: Marcel Driesman
Built: 1929-1932

This building, which is a mix of Art Deco and Modernism, was built for a Flemish operetta theatre, called the Lunatheater, on the site of a former theme park. The building, part of which extends along the canal, had a 2,000-seat theatre, a café, a meeting room, offices and 42 apartments. Unfortunately the theatre was forced to close after just two seasons as its director, Ernest Kindermans, died two weeks after the opening in October 1932.

In the Forties and Fifties, the theatre reopened, under a new name, the ABC, before becoming a carpet shop in the Sixties, which closed when the works on the construction of the Brussels underground started. In 1988, l'Immobilière moderne acquired the rundown building. Philippe de Hullu was tasked with the renovation, which was co-funded by the Ministry of Flemish Culture. The building reopened in 1993 and is now used by the Kaaitheater for its dance and theatre productions as well as various other productions. The ground floor has a café while the upper floors are home to various Flemish cultural associations. There are also a few apartments for artists. The main façade has a symmetrical design, and is built around a central axis, capped with a cylindrical element. The white rendered central spans contrast with the brick façades of the two lateral spans, which are aligned with the adjoining buildings.

The walk continues in the maritime quarter, which was where the old port of Brussels was situated. The canal that connects the city with the north of the country and that extends into the city with a number of docks, or the actual port, was inaugurated in 1561. At the end of the nineteenth century, the docks were gradually filled in and the port activities moved out of the Pentagon. The existing layout of these roads and their names refer to the former quays and docks.

Boulevard d'Ypres and boulevard de Dixmude were built after bassin du Commerce was filled in 1910-1911, on the former site of the Grand Entrepôt or large warehouse. The buildings along these avenues date from the 1920s. These are mixed-usage buildings, with medium-comfort apartments on the upper floors and large warehouses on the ground floors, which were used by fruit and vegetable wholesalers for the most part. This sector, which harks back to the earlier port activities, still has a large presence here today.

On the corner of boulevard de Dixmude (6-22), boulevard d'Ypres (68-80) and boulevard du Neuvième de Ligne (39-43), you will spot the Halles des Producteurs (arch. Arthur François, 1924), a mixed-usage Beaux-Arts building with a market hall on the ground floor and apartments on the upper floors. The Beaux-Arts style was very popular with bourgeois customers in Brussels from 1905 until 1930 and was inspired by eighteenth-century French styles. (listed 29/1/1998).

◀ Kaaitheater

5/ HALLES AMERICA

21-29, BOULEVARD DE DIXMUDE, 1000 BRUSSELS

Architect: Fernand Petit, with Jacques Obozinski
Built: 1925-1926
Listed: 29/1/1998

This mixed-usage building, which was built when the two architects were still associates, combines a retail function with housing and was signed by Fernand Petit (1885-1955). Petit, who designed various villas and houses in Brussels in the Twenties and Thirties, also built several larger buildings, like the Paul & Cousin garage (239, chaussée de Charleroi in Saint Gilles, 1927) and gare du Midi/Midi Station (1935-1952), applying the modernist principles in his designs.

The white stone and brick building stands out because of the rather simple and solid Art Deco style. It consists of a large, five-floor building and a smaller building with just three floors. It was originally built for a company called America et Cie, which was established in 1868 and which traded in fruit, vegetables, poultry, game and flowers. The ground floor of the main building, with its large skylight, was used as a covered market hall, with a sales floor that was lined with stalls, for the buyers. Trucks drove in through the large metal doors, which have since been renovated, and which define the façade's design. The vast ground floor was used as a warehouse. There were a few apartments, which were rented out, and offices on the upper floors. Buyers met in the café on the ground floor of the smaller building. The façade of the main building is symmetrical and built around an imposing entrance span, with a stairwell. It is punctuated by various vertical spans, that protrude slightly and which are all capped with white stone. The sawtooth profile of the white stone also returns in the white stone window aprons/sills.

▼ Halles America

6/ RETAIL AND APARTMENT BUILDING

34-36, BOULEVARD D'YPRES, 1000 BRUSSELS

Architect: Émile De Boelpaepe
Built: 1935

As the sign with the initials GKF and the monumental frieze with Art Deco lettering indicate, this building was commissioned by a company called Gérard Koninckx Frères, a wholesaler of bananas and oranges. The company already owned two similar buildings in the neighbourhood. The wholesale operation occupied the ground floor, the cellar levels, the first two floors and the mezzanine. The upper floors, two of which are slightly set back, comprised medium-comfort apartments, which were rented out. Trucks could enter the building on its open ground floor level. On either side of the monumental entrance, two small doors led to the upper floors. The left door gave access to the apartments, while the right door led to the offices. The white stone and faux stone façade has a very strong rhythm, with curved spans and columns with gilded capitals, that are decorated with banaas and oranges, extending across all four floors.

▼ Immeuble de commerce et à appartements, bd d'Ypres 34-36

The façades of the two Art Deco apartment buildings at 7-9, Boulevard d'Ypres and 6-8, quai du Commerce 6-8, which share a warehouse on the ground floor, are quite similar (arch. R. Teughels, 1933). The organisation of the buildings is very straightforward, with two apartments on either side of the central stairwell, on every floor. The stairwell is capped with a cylindrical mast, with two discs on top of it. There is an awning over each entrance that is capped with a volute pattern, bearing the initials of the original owner, i.e., Pierre Commerman, a wholesaler of fruit and vegetables. The palm leaf motifs of the wrought iron doors and the carved panel under the ground floor window, on the side of quai du Commerce, refer to the goods that were originally sold here.

7/ APARTMENT BUILDING

20-22, QUAI DU COMMERCE, 1000 BRUSSELS

Architect: Gérald Vuille
Built: 1928

This Art Deco apartment building, which was built for the representative of a Swiss company specialising in machines for the graphic arts, looks posher, largely because of its size and the decoration of its façade. The building had a concierge apartment and offices on the ground floor. There are three semicircular arched entrances on the ground floor, with a workshop in the cellar, with access for motorised vehicles. The two apartments on each floor had a large living and dining room and one or two bedrooms. Each apartment also had a maid's room on the seventh floor. The façade, in red brick, blue stone (base), white stone and faux stone, is very typical of this style. The ironwork of the balconies and the front door features stylised motifs. The second, third and fourth floor are especially eye-catching as they look more monumental than the rest of the building. They are linked by colossal pilasters with geometric motifs and carved capitals, depicting pairs of crouched Atlanteans who sit back to back. The three floors also have two spans with trapezoidal bow-windows, on either side of the central span with its balconies.

21-25, quai du Commerce, a rather massive brick Art Deco building, was built for a merchant who sold raincoats and gabardines (arch. A. and H. Vandaele, 1931). The building is punctuated vertically by bow windows on four floors, clad with faux stone. Another floor was added in 1934. Originally the plans provided for shops and/or a café on the ground floor and three apartments on every floor.

13-19, quai du Commerce 13-19, a modernist corner building, was built by Fernand Petit for the America et Cie company (1932), like the Halles America. The ground floor and cellar were transformed into a garage and warehouses, with three or four apartments on the upper floors. The somewhat massive façade has slightly recessed spans. The decoration is very simple, using various different materials: with bands of faux stone cladding for the window aprons and sills and masonry at the level of the windows. The building adjoins a large project of 80 social housing apartments with similar façades (2-10, quai du Chantier and 4-8, rue du Chantier), which was built by F. Petit for Foyer Bruxellois in 1936-1937.

▸ Apartment building, 20-22, quai du Commerce

8/ FORÊT D'HOUTHULST SOCIAL HOUSING PROJECT

2-12, BOULEVARD D'YPRES AND 1-17, RUE DE LA FORÊT D'HOUTHULST, 1000 BRUSSELS

Architect: Joseph Van Neck
Built: 1922-1924

This social housing project, and its identical counterpart on the corner of boulevard de Dixmude (1-13) and rue de la Forêt d'Houthulst (27-37) was built by Joseph Van Neck (1880-1959), who is perhaps better known for his architectural contribution to several international and world fairs (more specifically the 1935 fair in Brussels for which he built the Grand Palace on the Heysel) and as a lecturer and director of the Academy of Brussels (1907-1948). The two projects were built around an older building, i.e., the Semet-Solvay Foundation (19-25, rue de la Forêt d'Houthulst), by the same architect, built in 1913-1916 for the city of Brussels, at the instigation and with funding of the philanthropist Semet-Solvay. At the time, housing for the poorest in Brussels was built by the municipalities or philanthropic organisations. This changed after World War I, when the authorities sought to solve the housing crisis. In March 1922, the City of Brussels established Foyer Bruxellois, which took over from the Semet-Solvay Foundation and which built the Forêt d'Houthulst project. It has 102 apartments, 19 shops and a large interior courtyard. All the apartments had a small laundry-kitchen, a family room, a toilet, a terrace and one to four bedrooms. The apartments were very popular with large households (4 to 8 people). The first tenants included many labourers, junior employees as well as police officers. These low-cost buildings look rather simple. The corners feature turrets, surmounted by a pyramid-shaped roof, to ensure the project blended in with the other buildings in the neighbourhood, including mixed-usage and bourgeois buildings.

◀ Semet-Solvay Foundation, 19-25, rue de la Forêt d'Houthulst

▶ Social housing complex Forêt d'Houthulst, corner of rue de la Forêt d'Houthulst and bd d'Ypres

TITANIC

9/ APARTMENT BUILDING
10-32, RUE DU MARCHÉ AUX PORCS AND 2, RUE LOCQUENGHIEN, 1000 BRUSSELS

Architects: L. Muller and A. Servais
Built: 1935

The press hailed the construction of this investment property, *which combined the double requirements of any undertaking of this kind in an excellent fashion. It ensured the best return on the invested capital on the economic level while providing medium-priced rentals with an excellent level of habitability, hygiene, comfort and harmony on the social level. The architects (...) succeeded in reconciling these two principles while also obtaining a nice result.*[1] The unusual height of this vast functionalist building meant that a derogation had to be requested. It was subdivided into eight shops, ninety apartments (nine on every floor, around four stairwells with a lift) and a concierge's apartment. The building's massive appearance is softened by the alternating colours of the materials used to clad the façade, i.e., blue stone, polished green Labrador granite, Boom brick and faux white stone. The finish of the common areas and apartments is equally meticulous. Each apartment, with one or two rooms, had a bathroom, a fitted kitchen, a terrace and a living room. The corner apartments, which are the nicest, have plenty of light thanks to the seven adjoining windows, with sweeping views. It should be noted that the original plans provided for the addition of a special area in the cellar for carpet beating!

We continue our walk down rue Léon Lepage, a wide curved street, which was built in 1912 and parcelled up from the Twenties onwards, where we come upon a nice set of apartment buildings with Art Deco façades.

At No. 34, a simple apartment building (arch. A. Vandaele, 1931-1932) with a faux stone façade was built for a hat factory that was also based in rue Lepage, called Agnès, in order to provide its employees *with small comfortable apartments at advantageous prices so they could work effectively, thereby reducing the additional cost and fatigue to a minimum.*[2]

At No. 33-35, the former reformed church, a brick building with a few white and blue stone elements, was built to the plans of an Amsterdam-based architect called T. Kuypers (1927). The tower to the left housed the presbytery and the vicar's residence while the church proper was located in the wider, gabled right part of the building. The simple interior, in exposed brickwork under a wooden frame, was laid out in accordance with the reformed liturgy. The building has since been acquired by the Russian Orthodox community and was renamed Church of the Holy Trinity in 2003.

10/ FORMER WAREHOUSE

22-23, PLACE DU NOUVEAU MARCHÉ AUX GRAINS, 1000 BRUSSELS

Architect: Émile De Boelpaepe
Built: 1932

This functionalist building is the second building that Gérard Koninckx Frères had built in the neighbourhood. Originally, the building's cellar was used as a banana warehouse while the goods were unloaded and packed on the ground floor. The first floor, of double height, with a ramp, was used as a garage and the upper floors were occupied by warehouses and offices.

35-36, place du Nouveau Marché aux Grains, an Art Deco building (arch. J. Van der Linden, 1932) of which the ground floor was originally used by a fruit trader, with apartments on the upper floors. Two polychrome ceramic bas-reliefs on the façade refer to the building's former usage, featuring a black man's head between banana bunches and oranges.

85-101, rue Dansaert, a set of four buildings with apartments and businesses (arch. Louis Duhayon and Marcel Julien, 1924-1929), built around the same time as Saillant de l'Yser, by the SBI, stands out because of the original top of the building. A series of monumental dormers with curved and carved pediments sit atop the attic roof. This Beaux-Arts building comprised apartments for sale and businesses.

◂ Former warehouse, 22-23, place du Nouveau Marché aux Grains

11/ RETAIL AND APARTMENT BUILDING

75-79, RUE ANTOINE DANSAERT AND 7-11 RUE DU VIEUX MARCHÉ AUX GRAINS, 1000 BRUSSELS

Architect: Eugène Dhuicque
Built: 1927-1928
Listed: 26/3/1998

This Art Deco building, which combined businesses, warehouses and apartments in a rational manner, is the first building which Gérard Koninckx Frères built in the neighbourhood. Its size points to the flourishing exotic fruit trade after overseas trade picked up again following World War I. It was built by the architect Eugène Dhuicque (1877-1955), whose work is largely in the Art Deco style and who was influenced by the French example.

Originally, the ground floor, the covered interior courtyard and the large cellars were used as a warehouse, offices and shops. The trucks drove up to the loading quays through the two carriage entrances, one of which no longer exists. There were three investment properties/apartments on each floor, arranged around two separate stairwells, one of which also had a servant's staircase. Some of these comfortable apartments, with large family rooms, had a separate servant's entrance. The façade's rather classic decoration scheme combines blue stone for the base, cream-coloured brick and white stone. The highly colourful glazed sandstone frieze, on the attic floor and the dormers, makes it so original. It features orange trees and large banana leaves, with banana bunches between them, in large yellow spots. The frieze, which refers to the flourishing business of Gérard Koninckx Frères, was produced by the Parisian ceramic artist Dhomme, after cartoons by the Belgian painter Armand Paulis.

20-24, place du Vieux Marché aux Grains, an imposing functionalist investment property (1931) was subdivided into offices and apartments. The curved façade emphasises the building's horizontality.

◀ Retail and apartment building, corner of rue A. Dansaert and rue du Vieux Marché aux Grains

12/ L'ARCHIDUC

6, RUE ANTOINE DANSAERT, 1000 BRUSSELS

Architect: Franz Van Ruyskensvelde
Renovated: 1937
Listed: 3/3/2011

This superb Art Deco bar, which opened in 1937 in a late nineteenth-century building, is still one of the hot-spots of Brussels nightlife. Its sleek design, the two round columns, the mezzanine and the bar with its curved shape are reminiscent of the shape of an ocean liner, which was a very trendy design and architectural motif in the interwar period. The bar's first owner was a lady named Madame Alice (hence the letter A on the entrance door). At the time, it was a popular place where couples could secretly meet. The dark wood panelling, the chrome elements and the indirect lighting all add to the cozy atmosphere.

In 1953, the bar passed into the hands of the musician Stan Brenders, who transformed it into Brussels' leading jazz bar. Here you could listen to live piano music, often in famous company. Brenders was inspired by New Orleans jazz and performed with several famous bands, before establishing the Jazz Orchestra of the National Radio Broadcasting Institute in 1936. Upon his death, in 1969, his wife took over, leaving the Archiduc in the capable hands of Jean-Louis and Nathalie Hennart in 1985. They have continued to work in the spirit of Stan Brenders, continuing the wonderful piano bar tradition.

▼ L'Archiduc

THIRD WALK

THE CITY CENTRE

FROM PRÉVOYANCE SOCIALE TO SAINT-PIERRE UNIVERSITY HOSPITAL AND FROM THE CENTRE FOR FINE ARTS TO THE RVS BUILDING

We will discover the diversity of the buildings that were built in the Pentagon during the interwar period in two loops. They also point to the dynamism and the progressive tertiarisation of this neighbourhood during this period, with office and retail buildings, hospitals, hotels, recreation or cultural centres... Following the struggle for emancipation, everyone finally had access to leisure activities after World War I, leading to the construction of buildings for culture, popular entertainment and sport. They include the Centre for Fine Arts, cinemas, cafés, swimming pools... The authorities hoped to improve the quality of life of the population as a whole by building schools and hospitals. The success of the Belgian Workers' Party (socialist party) manifested itself in modernist buildings, like the offices of Prévoyance Sociale, a health insurance fund, or the printing plant of the newspaper *Le Peuple*. The first loop connects Prévoyance Sociale, in Anderlecht with Hôpital Saint-Pierre in the Marolles neighbourhood. The second loop focuses on a series of commercial buildings, hotels and cafés, around the avenues in the centre and runs from the Centre for Fine Arts to the RVS building.

◂ Prévoyance Sociale, square de l'Aviation, the landing between the ground floor and the mezzanine

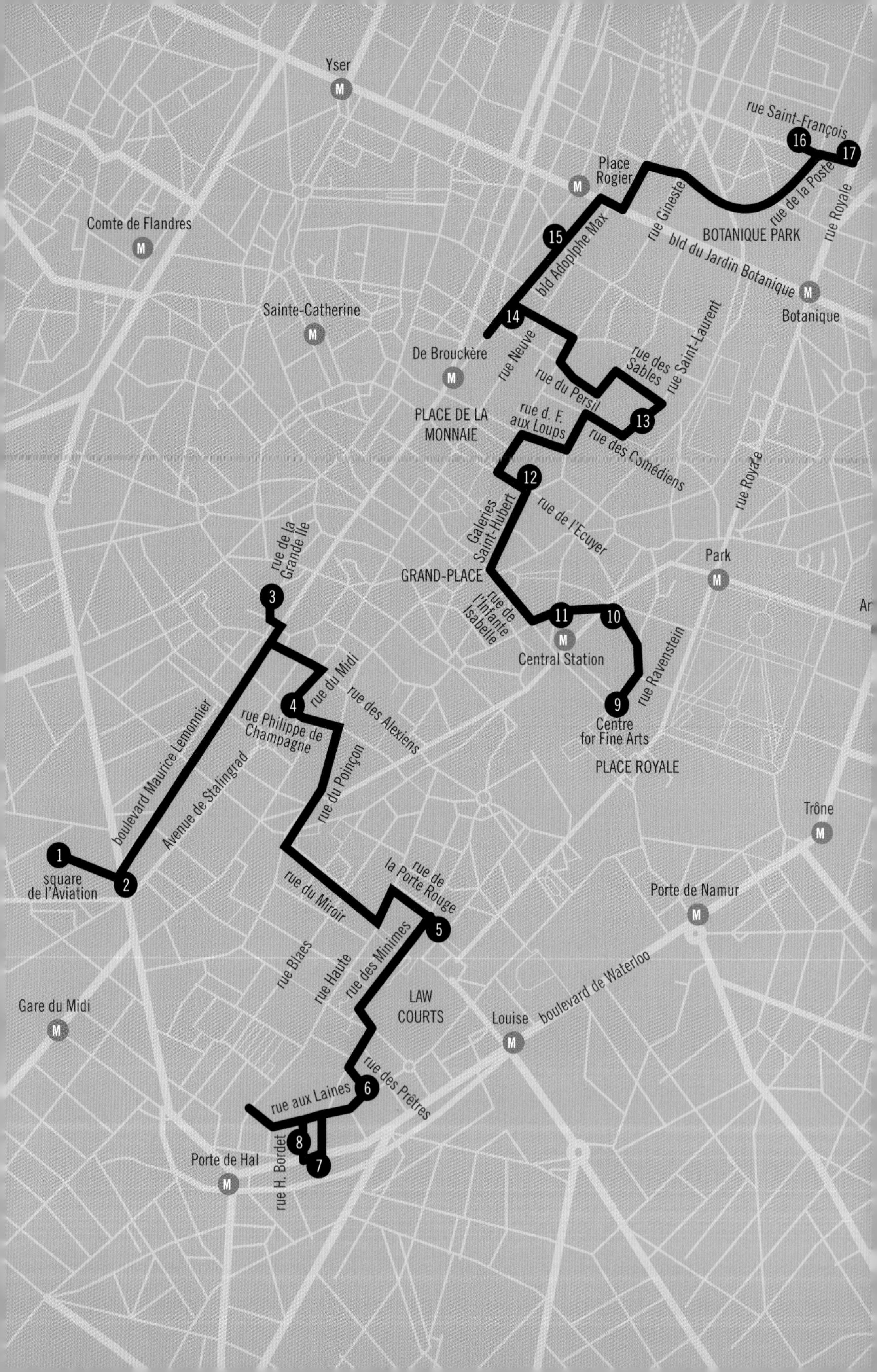

Yser
rue Saint-François
16
17
Place Rogier
rue Gineste
rue de la Poste
rue Royale
BOTANIQUE PARK
bld du Jardin Botanique
Botanique
Comte de Flandres
15
bld Adoplphe Max
Sainte-Catherine
14
De Brouckère
rue Neuve
rue des Sables
rue Saint-Laurent
rue du Persil
PLACE DE LA MONNAIE
rue d. F. aux Loups
13
rue des Comédiens
rue Royale
12
Galeries Saint-Hubert
rue de l'Ecuyer
rue de la Grande Ile
GRAND-PLACE
Park
Ar
3
rue de l'Infante Isabelle
11
10
Central Station
rue Ravenstein
9
Centre for Fine Arts
PLACE ROYALE
rue du Midi
4
rue des Alexiens
rue Philippe de Champagne
boulevard Maurice Lemonnier
Avenue de Stalingrad
rue du Poinçon
Trône
1
2
square de l'Aviation
rue de la Porte Rouge
rue du Miroir
5
Porte de Namur
rue Blaes
rue Haute
rue des Minimes
LAW COURTS
Gare du Midi
Louise
boulevard de Waterloo
rue des Prêtres
6
rue aux Laines
8
7
rue H. Bordet
Porte de Hal

01 LA PRÉVOYANCE SOCIALE
29-31, square de l'Aviation and 2-4, rue L. Crickx
1-3, 7-7A, rue de l'Autonomie and 4-10, rue L. Crickx,
1070 Anderlecht

02 FORMER EXPRESS-MIDI BREWERY
218, boulevard Maurice Lemonnier, 1000 Brussels

03 OLD DE RUYSSCHER PAPER MILL
39, rue de la Grande Île, 1000 Brussels

04 APARTMENT AND RETAIL BUILDING
36-40, rue Philippe de Champagne and 148, rue du Midi,
1000 Brussels

05 ROBERT CATTEAU SECONDARY SCHOOL
64-66, rue des Minimes, 1000 Brussels

06 FORMER ALBERT-ÉLISABETH DISPENDARY
15, rue des Prêtres, 1000 Brussels

07 FORMER MEDICAL SCHOOL OF THE UNIVERSITÉ LIBRE DE BRUXELLES
115, boulevard de Waterloo, 1000 Brussels

08 FORMER PAUL HÉGER AND JULES BORDET INSTITUTES
1-3, rue Héger-Bordet, 1000 Brussels

09 CENTRE FOR FINE ARTS
5-23, rue Ravenstein and 10, rue Royale, 1000 Brussels

10 SHELL BUILDING
48-70, rue Ravenstein and 47, Cantersteen, 1000 Brussels

11 CENTRAL STATION
carrefour de l'Europe, 1000 Brussels

12 FORMER VANDERBORGHT FRÈRES DEPARTMENT STORE
48-52, rue de l'Écuyer, 1000 Brussels

13 FORMER PRINTING PLANT OF *LE PEUPLE* NEWSPAPER
36-38, rue Saint-Laurent and 29-33-35, rue des Sables,
1000 Brussels

14 L'ESPÉRANCE
1-3, rue du Finistère, 1000 Brussels

15 PLAZA HOTEL
118-126, boulevard Adolphe Max, 1000 Brussels

16 BATHS OF SAINT-JOSSE-TEN-NOODE
23-27, rue Saint-François, 1210 Saint-Josse-ten-Noode

17 OLD RVS BUILDING
284, rue Royale, 1210 Saint-Josse-ten-Noode

FIRST LOOP

FROM PRÉVOYANCE SOCIALE TO SAINT-PIERRE UNIVERSITY HOSPITAL

1/ PRÉVOYANCE SOCIALE

OFFICE AND RESIDENTIAL BUILDING
29-31, SQUARE DE L'AVIATION AND 2-4, RUE L. CRICKX
1-3, 7-7A, RUE DE L'AUTONOMIE AND 4-10, RUE L. CRICKX, 1070 ANDERLECHT

Architects: Richard Pringiers, Fernand and Maxime Brunfaut
Built: 1911 and 1931-1932
Listed: 9/9/1993

Prévoyance Sociale, a cooperative insurance company, was founded under the umbrella of the Belgian Workers' Party (Parti Ouvrier belge, POB) in 1907. It was hugely successful from the outset. In 1911, it tasked R. Pringiers with the construction, on a corner parcel, of a six-floor building for its offices, as well as shops and apartments. Richard Pringiers (1869-1937), who had worked for Horta drawing the plans of the Maison du Peuple (1895-1899), was the POB's trusted architect. In 1905, he also built the offices of the *Le Peuple* newspaper for the party. In 1930, Prévoyance Sociale tasked Fernand and Maxime Brunfaut with the construction of two investment properties on the parcel behind the first building, along rue de l'Autonomie and rue Crickx. Soon the architects' intervention led to the modernisation and the raising of the building in square de l'Aviation and the construction, in this building block, of a tower for the party's archives. The two architects, who were closely linked to the party, spent fifty years constructing various buildings, in a modern style, which attested to the success of the workers' and cooperative movement in Belgium. They include community centres, social housing, garden cities, the offices of newspapers and party offices, the hospitals of the socialist health insurance fund, a sanatorium...

The young architect Fernand Brunfaut (1886-1972) did work placements with several leading architects who contributed to the development of this socialist architecture. He also worked on the plans of Brugmann Hospital under Horta's lead. He came to politics relatively early, and worked as an architect and socialist representative until the Thirties. After this, he focused exclusively on his political career. As an MP, he was one of the main defenders of the North-South railway junction and the author of a bill, the Brunfaut Act (1949), on the funding of social housing policies. Maxime Brunfaut (1909-2003) went to work for his father as of 1929, and soon played a vital role in the construction of projects with a more machinist aesthetic, influenced by the ocean liner style or avant-garde painting... In the Fifties, he built Central Station and the new Brussels Airport in Zaventem. In 1957, after Prévoyance Sociale moved out, the State acquired the corner building and tower. They were restored and then occupied, from 2004 onwards, by the War Victims Service, on the upper floors, and the Centre d'Études et de Documentation Guerre et Sociétés contemporaines (Documentation and research centre on war and contemporary societies, CEGES), on the lower floors. During the renovation in 1931-1932, the Brunfauts made sure not to alter the building's familiar appearance, by adding a floor (to this end the cladding of the upper floor and the glass dome were completely disassembled and moved up one floor). The ground floor façades were completely renovated. The materials used and the style foreshadow those of the large hall. The mezzanine and first floor underwent less radical changes, to assure a transition to the upper floors which remained unchanged. A bas-relief by Dolf Ledel (1893-1976) representing Prévoyance Sociale or social security, was installed above the main entrance: a man protects a woman and her child by raising his shield to the sky from where stones fall. This sculptor knew the Brunfauts well and was familiar with the socialist ideals. Three bronze double doors, which are protected by a flat awning, lead to the entrance hall, which has two levels, with a panoramic lift in the centre. A gallery on the mezzanine emphasises the hall's aerodynamic shape. The many chromed elements, the blueish walls, the polished marble, the vibrant blue of the enamels and the door frames all make this space look very modern. The first floor, where the directors' offices were located, was luxuriously decorated, with furniture by Maxime Brunfaut. The office walls were panelled with precious wood and the floors covered with carpets with dynamic designs. The other offices were on the upper floors, which were all laid out as large landscape offices with plenty of light. The two investment properties, which were built in 1931-1932 at the rear of the corner building, along rue de l'Autonomie and rue Crickx, had all the mod cons that you would have found in apartment buildings for the lower middle class: a maid's room, a rubbish chute, a dumbwaiter, a lift, a rooftop terrace... The red brick façades, which resemble each other, have vertical granito promontories, which separate the various spans. They are all decorated with sculptures by Dolf Ledel: a panel symbolising social security on the ground floor of rue de l'Autonomie and, at the top of each façade, two large figures symbolising architecture and the metal industry. A triangular tower, with eight floors, was built, to be used as an archive depot, in the building block, in the space between the two buildings, just six metres from their rear façade.

◀ Prévoyance Sociale, main façade in square de l'Aviation

▼ Prévoyance Sociale, entrance hall

2/ OLD EXPRESS-MIDI BREWERY

218, BOULEVARD MAURICE LEMONNIER, 1000 BRUXELLES

Architects: Adrien and Yvan Blomme
Built: 1934
Listed: 3/3/2011

This corner building, with its curved façade, which was built just a stone's throw from gare du Midi for the Caulier brewery, mainly served as an advertisement for its PERLE 28 beer. This figure referred to the quantity of malted barley in the beer, i.e., 28 kilos for every 100 litres. The inscription in blue and red ceramics stands out against the yellow brick façade.

This functionalist building had a café on the ground floor, with a wide, open storefront. The bar keeper lived on the mezzanine. Light flowed into the events venue on the upper floor through the many windows, which were accentuated in the façade by small black bricks.

▼ Old Express-Midi brewery

3/ OLD DE RUYSSCHER PAPER MILL

39, RUE DE LA GRANDE ÎLE, 1000 BRUSSELS

Architect: Eugène Dhuicque
Built: 1924-1927

This imposing corner building is part of a group of three buildings that were occupied at one time by the De Ruysscher paper mill. The other sections date from 1905 and 1949 respectively. Nowadays, the building is occupied by the Anneessens-Funck Institute. This Art Deco building, with four floors and a concrete structure, clad with yellow bricks, has a monumental entrance, in the shape of a basket handle. The awning is decorated with polychrome ceramics. The portal is surmounted by a medallion with the monogramme CDR, surrounded by symbols of commerce and industry and two horns of plenty. Two colossal pillars, whose sculpted decorative volutes frame a pediment with a flower frieze, add a monumental touch to the façade.

Do take a look at the entrance hall, with its walls and pillars clad with ceramics, its marble floor, the stained-glass window by Armand Paulis... The hall leads to an exhibition gallery and offices, on the ground floor. The workshops were on the upper floors.

▸ Old De Ruysscher paper mill

4/ APARTMENT AND RETAIL BUILDING
36-40, RUE PHILIPPE DE CHAMPAGNE AND 148, RUE DU MIDI, 1000 BRUSSELS

Architect: Léon Jean Joseph Govaerts
Built: 1927

This building is a late work by Léon J. J. Govaerts (1860-1930, not to be confused with his nephew, who had the same name). He designed buildings in all the styles that were fashionable from the 1880s to the 1930s! He started by working in Art Nouveau, designing social housing, before becoming interested in Art Deco. This apartment building with a ground floor shop is the result of the renovation of four nineteenth-century houses. Although the stained-glass window has since been replaced, your gaze is still automatically drawn to the corner of the building, which is all glass and squares. The façade in faux white stone, with its elegant decoration, has a vertical rhythm, thanks to the many spans, one of which protrudes from the building, in rue Philippe de Champagne. Its verticality is offset by the horizontality of the overhanging cornice and, on the side of rue Philippe de Champagne, by the uppermost floor, which is set back. Two trapezoidal balconies, on either side of the glass window, are supported by Cubist consoles. The door, which has been incorporated in an entrance with an awning and is surmounted by a bay window, features lovely geometric ironwork. The lift and granito floor with a geometric pattern in the entrance hall have been preserved. The apartment on the ground floor has its own entrance, on the street side. The apartments on the upper floors (two on each floor) were moderately comfortable.

At 37, rue du Poinçon, the Art Deco façade of a former printing plant, which has since been transformed into a private dwelling (arch. Henry Gilson, 1929), has a contrasting design, with brick and whitened concrete surfaces. The awning above the entrance protects two double entrance doors. One led to the sales room and the offices on the ground floor, while the other door led to the upper floors. A vast concrete warehouse was situated at the rear.

◀ Apartment and retail building, corner of rue Philippe de Champagne and rue du Midi

5/ ROBERT CATTEAU SECONDARY SCHOOL

64-66, RUE DES MINIMES, 1000 BRUSSELS

Architect: François Malfait
Built: 1923-1927

The plans for this secondary school, which was founded in the nineteenth century, were designed by François Malfait (1872-1955). From 1917 until 1942, he was employed as the municipal architect of the City of Brussels. As a result, he was asked to work on very different projects, including restoration projects. His own work, with polychrome brick façades, are characteristic of a sophisticated Art Deco style, which was inspired by the local tradition. The school's main entrance, at 49, rue Ernast Allard, resembles a pavilion with an awning. The more monumental Art Deco façade in rue des Minimes, symmetrically frames the central structure, which has been decorated with two groups of sculptures, representing allegories of Education, around a pediment with the school's name. The cleaning of the façade highlighted the quality craftsmanship of the red and yellow brick masonry, with blue stone elements. The buildings are grouped around two hillside playgrounds. The architect succeeded in incorporating this sloping parcel in a harmonious design, despite the many height restrictions he had to work with. The building could not block the view from place Poelaert in any way.

▾ Robert Catteau secondary school, façade in rue des Minimes

6/ FORMER ALBERT-ÉLISABETH DISPENSARY

15, RUE DES PRÊTRES, 1000 BRUSSELS

Architect: Jean De Ligne
Built: 1935

While the style of Jean De Ligne's (1890-1985) designs was more classical, his vernacular, from the Twenties onwards, became more modern. This dispensary was built for the Belgian Tuberculosis League, in a working-class neighbourhood, where this disease was still prevalent. It was situated near Hôpital Saint-Pierre, with which it collaborated, and was built to replace an outdated building.

The building makes no concessions in terms of decoration. Its horizontality is underscored by the flat roofs, the ribbon windows, the horizontal division of the window frames and the ironwork of the ground-floor windows with their simple design. The building's base is made of blue stone, while the rest of the façade has been finished with a green coating. The side façade in rue aux Laines breaks with the rigorous style of the main façade because of its irregular appearance. The austere entrance hall has retained several of its original elements including a bench, granito and ceramic elements... The building has since been converted into housing.

◂ Former Albert-Élisabeth dispensary

7/ FORMER MEDICAL SCHOOL OF THE UNIVERSITÉ LIBRE DE BRUXELLES

115, BOULEVARD DE WATERLOO, 1000 BRUSSELS

Architect: François Malfait
Built: 1924-1928

When the Université libre de Bruxelles moved to Solbosch in the Twenties, the Faculty of Medicine remained in the centre of the city, moving into a new building that was built with the support of the Rockefeller Foundation. This building, with its concrete structure and foundation, has brick and blue stone façades.

The main façade, whose verticality is accentuated by the colossal pillars, has a monumental portal: atlantics support the curved awning, with a frieze featuring foliage and fruit, which is surmounted by globes encircled by serpents. You need to look at this building from the side to understand its organisation. It has three parallel wings, which are connected by a wide central corridor. This arrangement allowed the architect to draw more natural light into the building given that the parcel was situated in between several narrow side streets. Originally the ground floor was occupied by practical laboratories and auditoriums. The labs and housing for the lab technicians were on the upper floors. The lab animals were housed on the top floor. Following the Faculty of Medicine's move to Anderlecht in 1981, the building was renovated. A new glazed floor was added, and it is now occupied by the offices of the Ministry of Justice.

◀ Former Medical School of the Université libre de Bruxelles

A NEW HOSPITAL ARCHITECTURE

In the early twentieth century, it soon became apparent that medical progress was inextricably linked with scientific research and a university education. As such, establishments for medical research and medical training were founded in the margin of these care institutions. The construction of the Medical School and the Héger-Bordet Institutes near Hôpital Saint-Pierre are a perfect illustration of this principle. Gradually, the City of Brussels undertook a complete renovation of its hospitals, which were deemed outdated by the medical profession. This led to the formulation of a new approach on the reception facilities and medical treatment of patients, which also had a significant influence on medical architecture. In the Twenties, the architect Jean-Baptiste Dewin soon emerged as the hospital expert, developing several new ideas. Dewin combined a perfect understanding of medical requirements in terms of hygiene, lighting, ventilation and distribution, with a welcoming setting, which was comfortable and reassuring for the patient. From 1922 until 1935, Dewin designed the Hôpital Saint-Pierre, travelling to the United States and Great Britain for inspiration. In the Thirties, modernist architecture became the most frequently used style for hospital buildings. The Héger and Bordet Institutes (1934-1939) and the Albert-Élisabeth dispensary (1935) are good examples of this. The white, smooth, immaculate, aseptic style of the operating theatre was extended to the rest of the building, which was stripped of any superfluous decorative elements.

8/ FORMER PAUL HÉGER AND JULES BORDET INSTITUTES

1-3, RUE HÉGER-BORDET, 1000 BRUSSELS

Architects: Gaston Brunfaut et Stanislas Jasinski
Built: 1934-1939

This functionalist complex, which is now called Institut Bordet, was built for the Commission d'Assistance publique de Bruxelles (the current public social welfare centre) and the Université libre de Bruxelles as a university centre for the study of cancer. It combined scientific and practical functions with research, analyses, diagnostics and treatment.

The building's design is the outcome of a collaboration between two architects, Stanislas Jasinski – who also built several apartment buildings in the city – and Gaston Brunfaut (1894-1974). The latter started to work as an architect under his older brother, Fernand Brunfaut. A passionate modernist, Brunfaut built houses and villas, social housing, hospitals, telephone switchboards and so on. In this many contributions, he stated that urban planning research was vital before starting to design a project. He believed that construction details only made sense if they were linked to the building's programme, which needed to be based on the client's requirements. The institutes were well ahead of their time, with their rather unique and plastic volumetry, its pared down façades that are clad with large white ceramic squares, its structure of concrete-clad metal beams, its sophisticated medical equipment, its ventilation and cooling. The buildings have two wings, with a semi-cylindrical tower in the middle, which is partly glazed. It has a slightly inclined ramp, which is practical for stretchers and which facilitated the entrance of visitors as well as a rapid evacuation. The T Wing, or Treatment Wing, along rue Héger-Bordet, with six floors, had exam rooms, labs, operating theatres, offices... The H Wing or Hospitalisation Wing, along rue aux Laines, had the best sunshine. It had 32 wards for 120 destitute patients and 39 rooms for 55 paying patients. An underground tunnel and glazed floating gallery (which no longer exists) connected the buildings to Hôpital Saint-Pierre.

The origins of Hôpital Saint-Pierre, a large complex between rue aux Laines and rue Haute, go back to the twelfth century. Originally a hospital for lepers, it became a general hospital, when Joseph II transferred the clinical courses of the Faculty of Medicine here in 1788. In 1806, Napoleon ordered that medical, surgery and pharmacy practicals be taught here. These courses, which were offered by the Medical School from 1824 onwards, led to the creation of the ULB's Faculty of Medicine. In the early Twenties, the City, the public social welfare centre and the ULB received support from the Rockefeller Foundation. They tasked the architect Jean-Baptiste Dewin with the rebuilding of the hospital. From 1926 until 1935, Dewin, who was inspired by Anglo-Saxon examples, built a tall hospital. The design facilitated a rapid circulation and a seamless collaboration between the various services. Over time, these buildings were no longer suited to new medical practices. In the early Nineties, construction started on a new hospital, which was completed in 2003. The entrance pavilion, on the corner of rue Haute and rue des Faisans, still exists as do the long buildings along rue Haute, which are now occupied by shops and the City of Brussels' public social welfare centre.

◂ Former Paul Héger and Jules Bordet Institutes

SECOND LOOP

FROM THE CENTRE FOR FINE ARTS TO THE OLD RVS BUILDING

9/ CENTRE FOR FINE ARTS

5-23, RUE RAVENSTEIN AND 10, RUE ROYALE, 1000 BRUSSELS

Architect: Victor Horta
Built: 1922-1928
Listed: 19/4/1977

Only a man with the talent and stature of Victor Horta could have pulled off the feat of constructing a building with such brio, on a parcel with so many technical constraints. The idea of building a cultural centre dated from before World War I. The city had neither an exhibition gallery, nor a concert hall at the time. The project was delayed by the war and afterwards by lack of funding. It finally kicked off in 1922 and was completed in 1928, with the support of the banker and patron of the arts Henry Le Bœuf and the City of Brussels. The irregular parcel, with a surface of 1 hectare, which is situated between rue Royale and rue Ravenstein on a large incline, was also defined by two easements. The first, which would go on to define the design, was a height restriction. The building could not block the view from place des Palais towards the city centre, meaning the building would have to be "buried" in the parcel. The second constraint, which was imposed by the City of Brussels, required the architect to add shopfronts on the side of rue Ravenstein. This explains the non-monumental façade of the building on which Victor Horta had the following to say: *A palace? Not in my mind. A simple arts centre, because I would never consent to calling a building which has shops in its main façade by this name.*[1] The building has various spaces, for a wide range of artistic activities. It is mainly renowned for its concert hall, the ovoid Henry Le Boeuf Hall, with its superb acoustics, which can seat an audience of 2,200 spectators. Victor Horta chose to focus on the interior organisation and the spatial arrangement, the distribution of the building's various functions and the combination of different volumes, like in all his other projects. He paid special attention to technical aspects, including ventilation, heating and the acoustics. The building's reinforced concrete structure was covered with steel beams and glass. This allowed Horta to create wide open spaces and draw in natural light. The blue stone façade has a rotunda on the corner, which serves as the main entrance to the building. The design features various spans, with identical modules and a geometric decoration. This Art Deco building has a simple, rather classical design. The interior, with its smooth walls, marble and parquet floors, has undergone many alterations since its inauguration. Following a recent restoration, the building has now been restored to its former glory. The round hall, which leads to a grand entrance hall and the Victor Horta Hall, a large hall with a glazed vault, which leads to the exhibition galleries, is usually open to the public. The Centre for Fine Arts soon became the epicentre of all arts and culture in the capital. It has continued to play this role over the decades, thanks to a dynamic management and a very diverse programme!

▸ Centre for Fine Arts, main entrance in rue Ravenstein

10/ SHELL BUILDING

48-70, RUE RAVENSTEIN AND 47, CANTERSTEEN, 1000 BRUSSELS

Architect: Alexis Dumont, with Marcel Van Goethem

Built: 1931-1934

In the early Thirties, Belgian Shell decided to build a new and functional building in the city centre, just a stone's throw from the future Central Station, for its offices. The project was entrusted to the architect Alexis Dumont (1877-1962). He wanted to fulfil the requirements of his client and the times, without abandoning tradition, which is why his style tended towards a monumental and modern classicism. Over time, his projects gradually became more restrained in style, with less ornamentation. This building has two wings, which are connected by a semi-circular volume, which is slightly set back, featuring a relief of the word SHELL. The strong incline of rue Ravenstein required the architect to build façades of differing heights around the rotunda. He originally also intended to build a 22-floor tower, behind the main building. This was never built, as the planning permit was denied. The Shell building is resolutely modern because of its reinforced concrete structure, its pared down exterior and technical innovations, including the ventilation, heating, insulation and so on. Originally, the design included shops on the ground floor, offices on the upper floors and a garage in the cellar. Shell occupied the offices in the Cantersteen wing, while the Ravenstein wing was rented out. On the side of Cantersteen, the seventh floor had a terrace, which you could access through the Shell company restaurant on the sixth floor. The façades are very simple. The ground floor is clad with polished Labrador granite. Its black colour contrasts with the bronze doors and window frames. The upper floors have been stripped of any ornamentation. The architect only added carved motifs in the blue stone overmantels between the windows of the four lower floors. The ribbon windows and flat roof only underscore the building's massive, horizontal appearance. The interior was designed to be comfortable, modern, practical, luminous and luxurious. Some offices had teak panelling, doors and furniture. The shops at the rear had a show window. You could access them from a gallery with travertine panelling, which connected the entrance halls of each wing and facilitated circulation within the building. While the gallery is still there, it is no longer used for its original purpose. The adjoining building at 26-46, rue Ravenstein, designed for Assurances Générales de Trieste, was built by the same architects (1934-1935). Alexis Dumont also designed the Ravenstein Gallery with his nephew Philippe Dumont (1954-1958).

▲ Shell Building

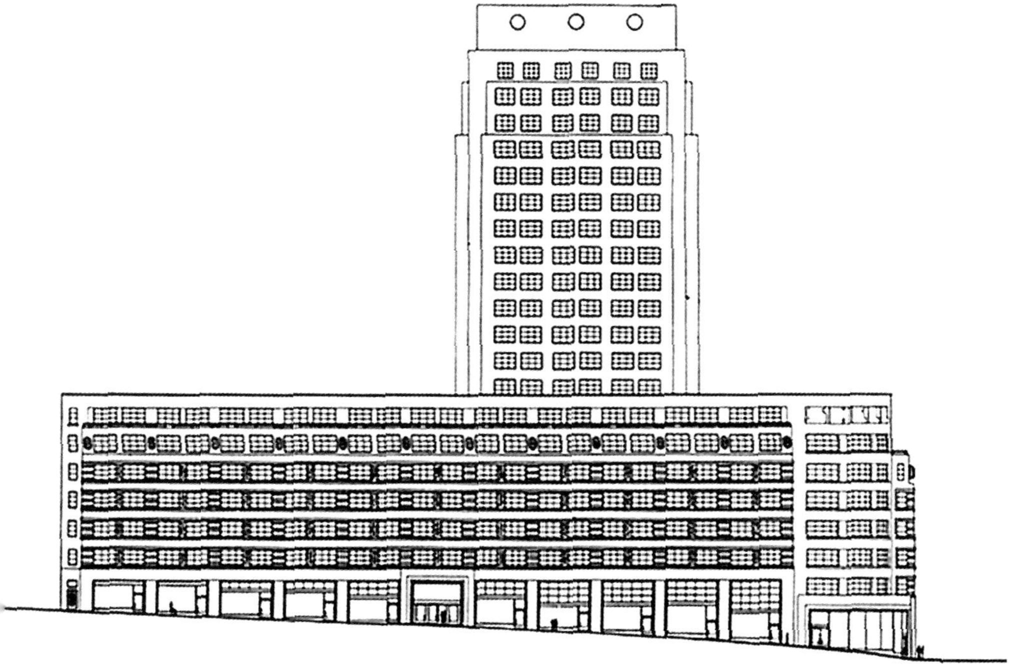

▲ Shell Building. Project including a tower that was never built. Taken from L'Émulation, No. 5, 1936, p. 80

11/ CENTRAL STATION

CARREFOUR DE L'EUROPE, 1000 BRUSSELS

Architects: Victor Horta and Maxime Brunfaut
Built: 1937-1952
Saved from demolition: 16/3/1995

Central Station was built on an irregularly shaped parcel, with a difference in altitude, which was the size of a building block. Victor Horta was tasked with building the station in 1910. His final designs were only given the green light in 1936. Construction lasted from 1937 until 1952. Maxime Brunfaut was in charge of the project from 1945 onwards, completing the station after Horta died in 1947.

The building, with its simple, functional architecture, which is clad with white stone, is the master architect's last and greatest achievement, combining classical influences with Art Deco. The main entrance is protected by a large awning, supported by four columns and surmounted by a concave façade with windows. Its vertical design contrasts with the horizontality of the lateral façades. Two bas-reliefs by Charles Leplae (1954) on either side of the entrance refer to the old Putterie neighbourhood. The great hall and the platform of the monumental staircase to the lower floors and the train platforms are lit from above, with daylight flowing in through the glass brick ceiling. The walls, which are panelled with travertine, are decorated with frescoes. The station was partly listed in 1995 and has since been restored by the architect Francis Metzger of Ma2.

◀ Central Station

We now arrive at the Galeries Saint-Hubert, which were inaugurated in 1847. At 30, Galerie de la Reine, Taverne du Passage (arch. Léon E. Govaerts and Alexis Van Vaerenbergh, 1928) has retained much of its original design.

THE NORTH-SOUTH JUNCTION

The history of Brussels' Central Station must be told in relation to the construction of the railway junction between North Station and Gare du Midi. For many decades, the idea of linking these stations had been floated and several solutions suggested. The principle of an underground junction, through the city centre, with several stops, was finally retained. In 1903, the City of Brussels and the State decided to demolish several old neighbourhoods, including Putterie, in order to free up the required space to build the junction and Central Station. The works started in 1911, were interrupted by World War I, restarted in 1935 and were finally completed in 1954. This required the moving of North Station and Midi Station, the construction of several new stations (Central Station, Congrès and Chapelle) and the demolition of 1,200 houses and several historic building blocks as well as the digging of a tunnel that literally cut the city in two. The reconstruction of the neighbourhoods around the junction happened in phases, from 1910 until 1960. It tackled separate blocks, starting with the upper part of the old historic neighbourhoods. The construction of the Centre for Fine Arts and the Shell Building date from this period. The neighbourhoods around the avenues that were built above the junction were only built in the Fifties and Sixties, in the international style. The area opposite Central Station remained unbuilt for many years. It was finally parcelled up in 1987. Associations are now investing to ensure a new urban mix, in neighbourhoods that are almost exclusively occupied by offices.

VICTOR HORTA (1861-1947)

In 1893, Victor Horta introduced a new architectural and decorative style, called Art Nouveau. Using metal structures and large skylights, this architect succeeded in drawing light into those parts of the house, where light did not usually enter. These structural innovations were combined with a new decorative language, drawing on the plant world for inspiration.

Horta considered architecture as a total project, designing furniture and decoration that was consistent with the space in which it was installed. Until World War I, he mainly built private dwellings, town houses, department stores, a hospital, a museum, a community centre (Maison du Peuple)... His wealthy clientele often espoused progressive ideas. From the early twentieth century onwards, he moved away from Art Nouveau, returning to the classical tradition instead. After World War I and some time in the United States, Horta gave free rein to more fertile spatial expression. The best example of his style at the time is the complex structure of the Centre for Fine Arts. During this time, he mainly built public buildings, in a more geometric style. He was also tasked with the design of Belgium's pavilion for the International Exhibition of Modern Decorative and Industrial Arts in Paris in 1925. He subsequently also designed plans for a company called Municipal Development, for the construction of real estate between the future Central Station and the Centre for Fine Arts. This mixed group of buildings included a tower, apartments, offices and a shopping gallery. The bankruptcy of the British company in 1928 meant the project was never completed. The Shell Building and the Ravenstein Gallery were built there instead. Horta's last feat was the construction of Central Station. He died before it was completed.

12/ OLD VANDERBORGHT FRÈRES DEPARTMENT STORE

48-52, RUE DE L'ÉCUYER, 1000 BRUSSELS

Built: 1932-1935 – Architects: Léon Emmanuel Govaerts and Alexis Van Vaerenbergh

In 1920, the Vanderborght brothers founded a decoration and furniture company, which proved quite successful. It had several shops and workshops in Belgium and also exported its designs.

In the early Thirties, the construction of spacious and modern shops, in the place of three neo-classical buildings in a building block between rue de l'Écuyer and rue du Fossé aux Loups, was entrusted to the architects Léon E. Govaerts (1881-*c.* 1970) and Alexis Van Vaerenbergh (1885-?). They became partners at the end of the Twenties working together until the early Fifties, building several Art Deco style interiors of shops, cafés and restaurants. They also built private dwellings, shops and swimming pools in a very pared down modernist style. In 1924-1928, they also built the van Buuren's house in Uccle. The Vanderborght department store was built in reinforced concrete around three glazed atriums. The highly functional atriums, which were stripped of any decoration, featured a five-floor façade, with a set-back top floor on the side of rue de l'Écuyer. The very horizontal design, with wide ribbon windows, travertine (which was subsequently replaced with a monochrome mosaic) and black Swedish granite caused quite a commotion, given that it was so different from the older buildings around it. A concrete canopy protected the display windows, which were beautifully lit. Customers entered here. Goods were displayed on several floors. Thanks to a system of sliding doors on rails, these resembled modular concrete plateaus.

◀ Old Vanderborght Frères department store

In the summertime, garden furniture was displayed on the rooftop terrace, where customers were also served tea. At the time it was built, the department store occupied a surface area of just under 16,000 m^2 (which was later increased to 30,000 m^2). We will later see the façade in rue du Fossé aux Loups where the employees entered. The Vanderborght company, which at one time employed a workforce of just under 1,000 employees, went bankrupt in 1980. The buildings remained vacant for quite some time, deteriorating rapidly. In 1998, la Monnaie/De Munt acquired the section along rue du Fossé aux Loups for its workshops. The City of Brussels, meanwhile, acquired the section in rue de l'Ecuyer, renting out to Artesia Bank (now Belfius Bank), which undertook its restoration. The building is currently unoccupied.

At 30-32, rue de l'Écuyer 30-32, on the corner of rue Léopold, an office and retail building (arch. Charles Verhelle, 1937) was built for La Mondiale, a French insurance company, as indicated by the inscription in the stone. The modernist design, with a concrete structure, is clad with Labrador granite and Savonnière stone.

On the opposite side of the street, an early modernist building at No. 41, which really deserves to be restored, was built in 1922 by Adrien Blomme for Élie Benezra, an Iranian carpet trader. This was the first time that this architect designed a commercial building. He chose to open out the shop onto the street, adding three semi-circular arched windows. The offices were on the upper floors, which are clad with white marble. (Saved from demolition: 23/4/1998).

At 39-41, rue du Fossé aux Loups, we walk along the rear façade of the Vanderborght company, which is currently occupied by the workshops of La Monnaie/De Munt. The building combines a large horizontal volume, with seven floors, to the left of a taller, vertical volume. The service staircase is situated in this tall glazed column. A symmetric, brick-clad wing was built to the right of this volume in 1961.

To the left and right, before turning onto rue Montagne aux Herbes Potagères, take some time to look at two more recent buildings, which are inspired by Art Deco. They are the former headquarters of the CGER (arch. Alfred Chambon, 1950-1953) with a white stone and copper façade, which is currently being renovated, and the Radisson Blu Hotel (arch. M. Jaspers and Atelier d'Art urbain, 1987-1989).

13/ FORMER PRINTING PLANT OF THE *LE PEUPLE* NEWSPAPER

36-38, RUE SAINT-LAURENT AND 29-33-35, RUE DES SABLES, 1000 BRUSSELS

Architects: Richard Pringiers, Fernand and Maxime Brunfaut – Built: 1905 and 1931-1932 – Listed: 26/4/1989

The architects who worked on this building are all architects who worked for the socialist movement at one time or another. *Le Peuple*, a socialist newspaper, which was founded in 1885, tasked Richard Pringiers with the construction of a building for its printing plant and workshops, its editorial offices and administration in 1905. He designed an Art Nouveau building at 33-35, rue des Sables. In 1923, the same architect built an extension in rue Saint-Laurent, which was replaced, in 1931, by the functionalist printing plant that was built by Fernand and Maxime Brunfaut (36-38, rue Saint-Laurent), which was again expanded in 1936-1937 (rue Saint-Laurent and 29, rue des Sables). The building became vacant in 1979, after the publication of *Le Peuple* as a separate newspaper ended. For 25 years, the building stood empty. It was acquired in 2001 by the representation of Asturias to the European Community, which wanted to occupy the section in rue Saint-Laurent. A private investor wanted to build apartments and shops in the section in rue des Sables. Following the renovation, the façades have been restored to their former glory. Unfortunately, the representation of Asturias has been forced to move out since then. The main building in rue Saint-Laurent has a symmetrical appearance, consisting of an almost square volume, which is almost entirely glazed, and a tower featuring the newspaper's name, which lights up at night and through which you can see the stairwell. The façade is clad with orange tiles, which contrast with the black tiles of the base, and which feature a bas-relief by Dolf Ledel, titled "Pour que le peuple lise" (So the people might read), in memory of Joseph Wauters, who managed the newspaper from 1910 until 1929. Some of the original interior elements have been preserved, such as the characteristic arches in the large printing hall. To the left of this building, you will see a functionalist annexe, built by Brunfauts in 1936-1937. The newspaper's first building is located at 33-35, rue des Sables, opposite the old Waucquez department store, which has since become the Belgian comic strip center (arch. V. Horta, 1903-1906). The ground floor (now the Marc Sleen Museum) and the counter hall, were renovated in a functionalist style in 1931. The awning and the flower beds accentuate the bay windows, adding a horizontal touch to the ground floor. This contrasts with the vertical line of the façade. Currently No. 29, which has large windows, and is clad with beige tiles, is occupied by an art gallery. It was originally part of the extension that was built in 1936-1937.

◀ Former printing plant of *Le Peuple* newspaper, façade in rue Saint-Laurent

14/ L'ESPÉRANCE

1-3, RUE DU FINISTÈRE, 1000 BRUSSELS

Architect: Léon Jean Joseph Govaerts
Renovated: 1930
Listed: 6/3/2008

You cannot take this walk without stopping at this brasserie, which was one of the architect's last designs! The marble façade, with a transom that is decorated with a geometric composition of printed glass, has been retained. Most of the original furnishings are also still in place, including the panelling, the benches, the ottomans, the low tables, the counter/bar, the stained-glass windows and so on. The establishment was also a hotel, with rooms that used to be decorated in the same style. For many years, this place, which is tucked away between Finistère church and the avenues, was a popular place with couples, who appreciated the cosy atmosphere and liked the discretion it offered.

Take a small detour to see Atlanta, at 5-9, bd Adolphe Max 5-9. This was the first hotel that Michel Polak built in Brussels (with Alfred Hoch, 1925-1929). The Art Deco-inspired building has a white stone façade, which is richly decorated with sculptures, with a wide curved gable. The ground floor features elaborate ironwork and clad with marble. On the ground floor there used to be a large tea room with a dance hall. The dining room in the cellar, which resembled an ocean liner in style, could accommodate up to 200 guests.

▾ L'Espérance

15/ PLAZA HOTEL

118-126, BOULEVARD ADOLPHE MAX, 1000 BRUSSELS

Architects: Michel Polak et Alfred Hoch
Built: 1928-1931
Cinema listed: 23/7/1992

Michel Polak's name is forever linked to the Résidence Palace and Villa Empain, but also to a series of Art Deco-inspired hotels. The architects were inspired by the design of the George V Hotel in Paris, for this large complex of three wings, arranged in an inverted U, with a cinema with 1,300 seats. The reinforced concrete façade, clad with white stone, is very pared down. It has a curved corner on the side of rue de Malines. The upper floors are gradually set back. The hotel was forced to close in 1976, reopening in 1996 after a long renovation. The cinema, which can be accessed from the avenue, features a sophisticated decorative scheme. The rectangular-shaped cinema, with a ground floor and balconies, faces a stage and a screen, with fake boxes on either side. The Spanish Renaissance decoration, which was very fashionable in the United States at the time, adds a Hollywood feel to the ensemble. The architect relied on avant-garde technology for the ventilation and acoustics so the sound of the films would not be heard in the hotel. In the early Eighties, a furniture store occupied the cinema, before it was renovated and incorporated in the hotel as an upscale events venue.
After the emergence of "talkies" in the early Twenties, cinema became one of the most popular entertainments for the masses. Several cinemas were built or modernised around the city. Many of these buildings were often decorated in a flamboyant Art Deco style, in line with the films that were screened here. In the Thirties, architects turned to a more austere style. Over time, many of these cinemas closed down or were converted. The Métropole (arch. Adrien Blomme, 1932) in rue Neuve, for example was renovated. UGC De Brouckère still retains the decoration of the old Eldorado cinema, which was inspired by African art (arch. Marcel Chabot, 1933, listed 28/4/1994).

▼ Former Plaza cinema

We now find ourselves in place Rogier where North Station was located during the interwar period. This also explains the many luxurious hotels around this neighbourhood. They include the Siru, originally called Nord Hôtel (arch. Marcel Chabot, 1932), on the corner of rue du Progrès and rue des Croisades, with its characteristic dome. A harbinger of Art Deco because of its geometric decoration, the Palace Hôtel (Crowne Plaza) was built in 1908-1909 and stands out because of the stylised caryatids that frame the windows of the mezzanine (arch. Antoine Pompe et Adhémar Lener). Hôtel Albert 1er, now the Hilton, was built by Michel Polak. The very simple Art Deco ornamentation consists of stylised floral motifs on the sixth floor and in the ironwork railings. Now let's walk around the Hilton and through Botanique Park to rue de la Poste. There we turn into the second street on the left.

▶ Plaza Hotel

HOTEL PLAZA

16/ BATHS OF SAINT-JOSSE-TEN-NOODE

23-27, RUE SAINT-FRANÇOIS, 1210 SAINT-JOSSE-TEN-NOODE

Architects: Jos Bytebier and Charles Schaessens
Built: 1933
Listed: 4/6/2009

This yellow brick, blue stone and French stone building in the Art Deco style features a bilingual inscription in an original font. Although the interior was partially renovated in the Sixties, it has retained many of its original characteristics including the row of cabins that opens out directly on the swimming pool. From the outset, the building had a swimming pool, Turkish steam baths and baths, which proved quite useful in a neighbourhood where many of the dwellings did not have a proper bathroom. The building is currently closed for renovation and is scheduled to reopen by the end of 2018. During the interwar period, physical exercise was encouraged by the authorities and by public initiatives. The idea was that sport was a source of hygiene and a good condition but it could also be a source of pleasure. The public became interested in sports thanks to events like the Antwerp Olympics of 1920 or because of media attention. The public flocked to races and sports competitions. This led to the construction of adapted infrastructure such as swimming pools, solariums, stadiums... The Joseph Mariën stadium (arch. Albert Callewaert, 1926), in chaussée de Bruxelles in Forest, for example was used by the Union Saint-Gilloise, or the Heysel stadium (arch. Joseph Van Neck, 1930), which has since made way for the new King Baudouin Stadium.

◀ Baths of Saint-Josse-ten-Noode

17/ OLD RVS BUILDING

284, RUE ROYALE, 1210 SAINT-JOSSE-TEN-NOODE

Architect: Jos Duijnstee
Built: 1936-1938
Listed: 3/3/1988

This functionalist building was constructed for the Rotterdamsche Verzekering Societeiten (RVS), a Dutch insurance company. In 1955, the building was extended at the rear, towards rue de la Poste, by the architect Charles Van Nueten. From 1962 until 1990, the building was occupied by a school before it was sold to a real estate developer. As it remained vacant for several years, it deteriorated. In 1997, SD WORX, a payroll company, acquired the building, undertaking its renovation while respecting its original aesthetic and taking into account new office requirements.
After SD WORX left, the building was acquired by the municipality of Saint-Josse-ten-Noode in 2017, to be used for its offices. The façades, with blue stone bases, which are finished in a light colour, have several colour accents, including stained-glass windows, the window frames and mosaics. On the side of rue Royale, the building features a central entrance, with a lintel with the letters RVS. The blue stone frame is edged with mosaics, which extend the line of the door's ironwork. The corner element, a glazed, luminous protruding enclosure, above the cornice, resembles a beacon, standing out among the classical buildings that line rue Royale. Originally the company's logo, with the initials RVS, was installed here. The lateral façade combines a series of vertical and horizontal elements, with volumes that protrude or are set back. Three openings, with stained glass windows, extend along the entire façade and are framed by protruding jambs, drawing light into the stairwell. From a stylistic perspective, this building refers to a style that is not very well-known in Belgium, which is called *the Cubist variant of the Amsterdam School.*[2] Its avant-garde allure was meant to accentuate the progressive views and image of the building's owners. The interior is organised in a functionalist manner, combining an open plan with reinforced concrete. The reception hall and the former office of the CEO still feature ceramic frescoes by Jaap Gidding, an artist of the Amsterdam school.

◀ Old RVS building

FOURTH WALK

THE COGHEN NEIGHBOURHOOD

ALTITUDE CENT TO THE HAERENS HOUSE

This walk connects St Augustine's Church with the neighbourhood around avenue Brugmann, leading up to avenue Coghen. These neighbourhoods were especially popular with real estate developers in the Thirties. As a result, there are several beautiful architectural ensembles here, such as square Coghen. While the houses that were built at the top end of avenue Coghen were often built in sets, some of the houses near avenue Brugmann are the result of close collaborations between a renowned architect and an informed client. A good example is the Dotremont House, which was built by L. H. De Koninck, and which was the first modernist house to be listed, in 1977.

◀ St Augustine's Church place de l'Altitude Cent

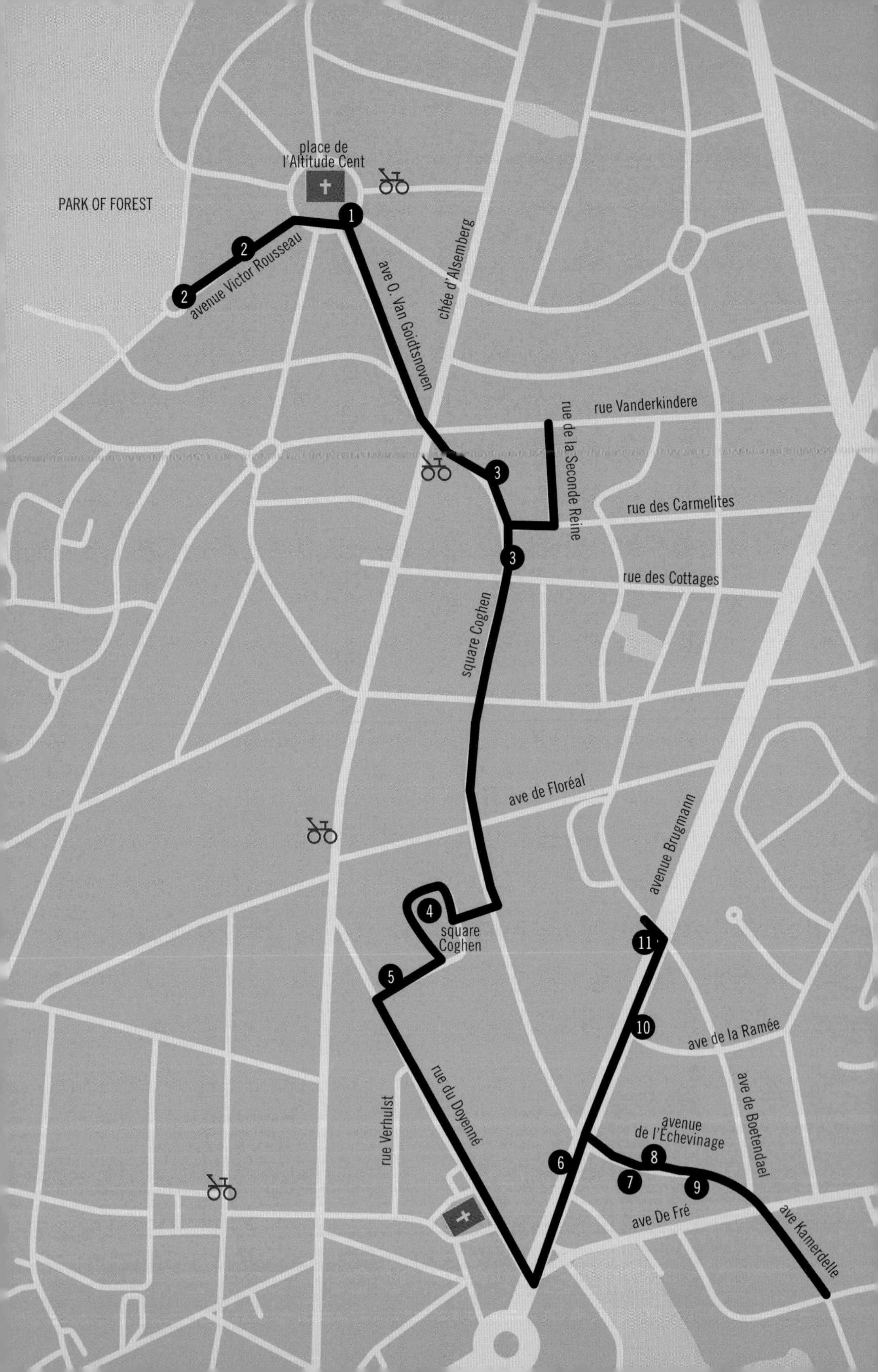

place de
l'Altitude Cent
PARK OF FOREST
1
2
2
avenue Victor Rousseau
ave O. Van Goidtsnoven
chée d'Alsemberg
rue Vanderkindere
rue de la Seconde Reine
3
3
rue des Carmelites
rue des Cottages
square Coghen
ave de Floréal
avenue Brugmann
4
square
Coghen
5
11
10
ave de la Ramée
rue du Doyenné
rue Verhulst
ave de Boetendael
avenue
de l'Échevinage
6
7
8
9
ave De Fré
ave Kamerdelle

01 **ST AUGUSTINE'S CHURCH**
place de l'Altitude Cent, 1190 Forest

02 **DWELLINGS**
11, 32, 33, 72-74, avenue Victor Rousseau, 1190 Forest

03 **DWELLINGS**
28, 40, 42, 59, 68, avenue Coghen, 1180 Uccle

04 **SQUARE COGHEN**

05 **GROUP OF DWELLINGS AND SHOP**
75 to 87, square Coghen, 1180 Uccle

06 **HOUSE**
491, avenue Brugmann, 1180 Uccle

07 **DOTREMONT HOUSE**
3, avenue de l'Échevinage, 1180 Uccle

08 **HOUSE**
16, avenue de l'Échevinage, 1180 Uccle

09 **FORMER PRIVATE HOME AND OFFICES OF THE ARCHITECT**
21, avenue de l'Échevinage, 1180 Uccle

10 **HAERENS HOTEL**
384, avenue Brugmann and 2, avenue de la Ramée, 1180 Uccle

11 **CLAIRE MAISON**
421, avenue Brugmann, 1180 Uccle

1/ ST AUGUSTINE'S CHURCH

PLACE DE L'ALTITUDE CENT, 1190 FOREST

Architects: Léon Guianotte and André Watteyne
Built: 1932-1936
Listed: 8/8/1988

In 1900, the main traffic arteries leading to the future place de l'Altitude Cent, which is the highest point in the city of Brussels, were laid out. The plans also provided for the construction of a church with a tower, that would be situated exactly in the centre of the eight streets that extended from the square. A first design, which was submitted in 1914, was not executed due to a lack of funds. In 1928, Léon Guianotte (1891-1976) and André Watteyne (1894-1971) designed plans for a church in concrete, an innovative and low-cost material.

The works were officially completed in the mid-Thirties but it took several years before the church was really finished. The coatings took until 1946 to finish, and were done using mediocre materials, as a result of which the external surfaces deteriorated. The coatings, which were too light, peeled off, causing the degradation of the concrete. At one point, the demolition order was on the table but the building was saved after it was listed and subsequently restored in 1996-1997. The symmetrical building is built around a central point and has a 50-metre tall tower. It has a Greek-cross plan (four arms of equal length), which is inserted in a circle. The church thus refers to tradition while having a modern design. The façades feature ridges, hollows, and reliefs, accentuating its overall Art Deco appearance. The church's structure, which was built using reinforced concrete, is obvious on the outside and inside. The concrete was solely used for the structure and for building the tower. The tower's exterior is made of reinforced concrete. Masonry was used for the elevations, right up to the roof/terraces. The interior's unconventional volume and slender tower are striking. The church's centre is shaped by four columns that support the beams on which the tower rests. The light in the church is yellow-orange, because of the light that falls in through the large stained-glass windows. A Via Crucis, which was designed by André Watteyne and carved in bas-relief by Oscar De Clerck, decorates the curved walls.

◄ St Augustine's Church

REINFORCED CONCRETE

Along with the churches of Saint John the Baptist in Molenbeek and St Susan's in Schaertbeek, St Augustine's Church is one of three religious buildings to be built in reinforced concrete in Brussels in the Thirties. Architects started using this material from the late nineteenth century onwards, but its use became more widespread from the interwar period onwards. Its plasticity, its ability to take on different shapes thanks to formwork, the speed of execution and its low cost, the availability of the materials needed to produce it and the fact that it was deemed very sturdy (at least in those days) played in its favour. Reinforced concrete offered builders of high-rise buildings another option. In Belgium, the architects of garden cities were the first to experiment with this material, setting the standard in concrete construction techniques, starting with Victor Bourgeois who built the Cité Moderne (1922), Huib Hoste and Kapelleveld (1923-1926)...

Reinforced concrete was subsequently used to build more prestigious buildings such as apartment buildings, hotels, churches and so on. The works of L.H. De Koninck, who continued to research techniques for using concrete in the construction of upper middle-class homes, are a good example. That said, using a relatively new and unknown material also resulted in problems as the quality of the work ultimately depended on several technical parameters. The materials used to produce concrete were not always of optimum quality, the mixes were not always correctly done, the metal frames were sometimes badly coated or badly installed, the concrete was sometimes badly protected... These defects accelerated the degradation of modernist buildings, many of which were demolished, renovated or, in the best-case scenario, restored.

2/ DWELLINGS

11, 32, 33, 72-74, AVENUE VICTOR ROUSSEAU, 1190 FOREST

Architect: François Van Meulecom
Built: 1924, 1923, undated, 1938

The work of François Van Meulecom (1889-1963) is very similar to that of Jean-Baptiste Dewin, with whom he collaborated for several years. He produced several upper middle-class houses and small apartment buildings in various Art Deco neighbourhoods around Brussels. He also built affordable housing, among others in Molenbeek. His upper middle-class houses, in an original Art Deco style, reveal his meticulous attention to design, his penchant for the picturesque and for symmetry. They look very comfortable and intimate. The architect added multiple porches, balconies, bow-windows, wrought iron elements, combining them with brick and stone in his façades, which featured colourful window frames or stained-glass windows.

36-42, avenue Rousseau, a group of modernist houses by Charles Colassin (1934). Their horizontal design is emphasised by the flat roofs, the cladding with elongated bricks and the continuous projection of the balconies and bow-windows. Unfortunately, the design has been altered by the addition of new window frames and doors.

▾ House, 72-74 av. V. Rousseau, arch. Fr. Van Meulecom

▾ Dwellings, 36-42, av. V. Rousseau arch. Ch. Colassin

3/ DWELLINGS

28, 40, 42, 59, 68, AVENUE COGHEN, 1180 UCCLE

Architect: Louis Tenaerts

Built: around 1935

Like Van Meulecom, Louis Tenaerts (1898-?) built several sets of houses, in various styles, usually in the Art Deco style. He was not an innovator, he did not take a new approach to the design of the interior volumes. His façades usually feature a series of recurrent elements, which he combined in various different ways every time. That said, he did contribute to the development of charming neighbourhoods such as this one. The majority of his – relatively unknown – activity is largely concentrated in Uccle and in the neighbourhoods of the second tier. He also often worked for the Comptoir immobilier belge, as is evident from the inscription C.I.B. arch., alongside his signature on many of his buildings. This housing authority built various investment properties and family homes. Below is our selection of the architect's works. There are plenty of others of course. No. 28 resembles a picturesque ocean liner. The entrance is surmounted by a semi cylindrical projection that extends along the entire height of the façade. The curve is accentuated by the overhanging cornice, the protruding windows and the awning over the entrance door. A pergola with horizontal wooden elements caps the second-floor terrace. No. 40 is quite similar. The horizontal wall sections under the windows and the rooftop terrace are shaped like a wave, connecting with the cylindrical shape of the lateral projection, while softening the protrusion and adding dynamism to the façade design. The window at No. 42 was replaced. Tenaerts liked to use black ceramic tile with white joints to clad the base. At No. 68, an elongated window with a neutral-coloured stained-glass window adds verticality to the façade and is offset by the horizontal lines of the awning over the entrance, the white joints and the protruding window casings. The flat roof also acts as a terrace.

34, rue de la Seconde Reine, a charming Art Deco façade, combining red brick with faux stone (arch. Guillaume Hebbelynck, 1931-1932).

▼ House, 28, av. Coghen, arch. L. Tenaerts

28

5, rue de la Seconde Reine, an original design by Tenaerts, with a striking stained-glass window with a diagonal design (1933-1934), through which you can see the light-drenched stairwell. The right span features a set of protruding elements, which accentuates the balcony and the entrance.

Now let's return to 82, avenue Coghen, to a house where the brick cladding points to the influence of the Amsterdam School (arch. Charles Van Nueten, 1929). The stained-glass windows and ironwork consist of inverted triangles.

At No. 85, a modernist house (arch. Gaston Brunfaut, 1935), with a somewhat traditional design, mainly because of the use of brick.

At No. 120, a house with modernist characteristics (arch. R. Delville 1935).

At No. 127 and 129, two designs by Pierre Verbruggen, which point to the transition in his work. At No. 127 (1927), the influence of the Amsterdam School, which influenced his early career, is still apparent. Just look at the brick cladding, the door and the windows with their small stained-glass panels, the small garden's wrought iron gate, which reprises the inverted triangle shape mentioned above. At No. 129 (1930), the architect created a more assertive modernist design. The building has been altered by a recent renovation.

◤ House entrance, 28, av. Coghen, arch. L. Tenaerts

◥ House, 28, av. Coghen, arch. L. Tenaerts

◣ House, 5, rue de la Seconde Reine, arch. L. Tenaerts

◢ House, 68, av. Coghen, arch. L. Tenaerts

▼ Dwellings, 127 and 129, av. Coghen, arch. P. Verbruggen

4/ SQUARE COGHEN

This more or less oval-shaped square is the only example in Brussels of a modern subdivision for a well-to-do group of people. Designed in 1929, on the site of the former Coghen property, it was developed in less than ten years, house by house, by the people who purchased the parcels, or in small groups, by the real estate developer, Baron Raoul de Limnander de Nieuwenhove. The architects took advantage of the sloping land to build several small front gardens and houses with cubic volumes, with rooftop terraces, and white façades with horizontal windows and protruding features. In many ways, this development is very similar to the garden cities of this era, sharing the same desire to establish a balance between architecture and nature, the intimate and closed character of the design, the smaller footprint of the single-family homes.

As you walk through square Coghen, you will spot two houses by Josse Franssen (1906-1990) at No. 9 (1935) and No. 11 (1929), which point to his penchant for superposed volumes, which is such a typical feature of this architect's work. The entrance of his personal home, at No. 11, is surmounted by a cantilevered roof overhang. Franssen, who greatly admired L.H. De Koninck, a proponent of rational architecture, built several houses and villas in Uccle during the interwar period. He subsequently went on to specialise in apartment buildings. No. 28 to 48 consists of a set of 10 houses by the architect Pierre Verbruggen (1933) at the request of Raoul de Limnander.

▼ Set of houses, 28-48, square Coghen arch. P. Verbruggen

5/ GROUP OF DWELLINGS AND SHOP

75 TO 87, SQUARE COGHEN, 1180 UCCLE

Architect: Louis Herman De Koninck
Built: 1935-1936

Philippe Dotremont was very satisfied with his first collaboration with De Koninck, which is why he decided to work with him again in 1935 on an apartment building/investment property on an elongated parcel, with a right of way, which he owned in square Coghen. The architect's project was particularly profitable as he designed an apartment building on the side of rue Doyenné as well as several housing blocks on both sides of the street. Only one side of the project was built, i.e., these six semi-detached houses and an apartment building with five apartments and a shop on the ground floor. While the houses at the top of the square are examples of a more attenuated Modernism, the designs of De Koninck are much more rigorous. The metallic tubular railings of the terraces refer to naval architecture with their curves softening these rather Cubist buildings. The porches resemble additional volumes that have been attached to the buildings and are protected by rectangular awnings. Originally, the window frames were painted a darker colour, which contrasted with the light concrete of the façades.

▼ House, 75, square Coghen, arch. L. H. De Koninck

66-68, rue Verhulst, let's stop to look at two houses built in 1925, by Lucien François (1894-1983). He received his training, by working for Fernand Bodson among others. He spent most of his career designing individual or collective housing. He also contributed to the Floréal garden city in Watermael-Boitsfort (1921-1922). Like Antoine Pompe, in whose footsteps he followed as a lecturer at La Cambre, he belonged to the school of modernists who refused styles but did not endorse the total elimination of any ornamentation whatsoever. The house at No. 68, with its geometric composition, is the only house to have retained its original features. The brick cladding, the washed concrete lintels and the blue stone emphasise the triangular shapes of the bow-window, the terrace and the awning over the entrance. The colourful stained glass of the window frames on the ground floor and the door is the original stained glass.

85, rue du Doyenné, an Art Deco shop window, which was built in 1935, on the ground floor of an eclectic building, for the ice-cream maker/baker Marcel Ottoy (arch. Simoens), combining materials such as marbrite glass, stained glass, chromed metal and polished wood. It is very rare to find Art Deco shop windows that are as well preserved as this one (listed: 8/10/1998).

▸ House, 68, rue Verhulst, arch. L. François

▾ Shop window, 85, rue du Doyenné, arch. Simoens

6/ HOUSE

491, AVENUE BRUGMANN, 1180 UCCLE

Architect: Pierre Verbruggen, with L.H. De Koninck
Built: 1925

Before World War I, Pierre Verbruggen (1886-1940) honed his skills by working as a designer for Paul Hamesse, where he became familiar with the style of the Viennese Secession. He also researched ever more economic solutions. After the war, he participated in the reconstruction of the country, set up his own firm, and built a series of houses in a style that is very similar to that of the Amsterdam School. He then turned towards a more assertive modernist style, something which is particularly evident in his design for the Ostend Maritime Academy, for which he won the Van de Ven prize in 1933. This house still points to the influence of the Viennese Secession. Have a look at the characteristic arches of the garage door and the porch, the symmetry and geometry, the decorative use of brick... The bow-window and terrace are surmounted by a frieze of terracotta tiles, flanked by two sculptures representing stylised pelicans.

◂ House, 491, av. Brugmann, arch. P. Verbruggen

7/ DOTREMONT HOUSE

3, AVENUE DE L'ÉCHEVINAGE, 1180 UCCLE

Architect: Louis Herman De Koninck
Built: 1932-1933
Listed: 13/4/1977

The factory owner Philippe Dotremont, who collected modern art, moved to Brussels in 1928 and asked Louis Herman De Konick to design him a house. While the architect had to make a huge effort to satisfy his demanding client, the resulting design is often considered his best. The simple, elegant and almost flat façade is made of a reinforced concrete panel that is about 15 cm thick, which is quite unique. The smooth plain appearance of many modernist buildings is the result of the use of a coating on a reinforced concrete structure, with brick filling. What you see here is not a coating proper, however. Instead the façade was bush-hammered after it dried. Using this technique meant the construction work had to be continuously supervised. If, during the casting and the tamping, the formwork was placed too close to the outer surface of the wall, the water infiltration could cause the formwork to corrode, resulting in the rapid degradation of the façade. While De Konick had a good understanding of building with concrete, many of his fellow architects did not. The house has a small front garden, with a tubular fence. A basin follows the line of the bow-window, the roof of which is then skilfully extended into an awning above the hollow entrance in the centre of the façade. The façade is asymmetrical, which only makes it look even more modern. The bow-window on the ground floor contrasts with the large bay window, with small panes on the second floor. The axis shifts, from the centre on the ground floor, to the left on the upper floors. The façade reveals the house's rather complex internal structure. The study/smoking room, where the ebony panelling has been retained, is situated behind the ground-floor bow-window.
This room, which was used to receive business contacts, still looks very traditional. The door gives out onto a modest hall, which leads to the living room, where the space fans out in several directions. In the centre, to the right, the space extends on two levels, and is surrounded on the upper floor, by a gallery with a staircase. To the left,

▼ Dotremont House

under the gallery, the dining area gives out into the kitchen. The vast living area looks out onto the garden. Here you can really see how modern this house is. The idea of combining rooms with different uses on two levels in one and the same volume was extremely modern, even though it was inspired by the designs of Victor Horta, albeit more radical in design. The bright, simple interior is equally striking. A few glass block walls draw the light into the very heart of the space. The banister of the staircase and the railing of the gallery are made of metal tubing. The first-floor gallery leads to two bedrooms on the street side and to the master bedroom on the garden side, with the adjoining bathroom and laundry room. There was one more room (which is now a bathroom) on the upper floor, with windows at the rear, and a gym, behind the large bay window in the façade. From there you could get to the roof terrace, which occupied the rest of the floor.

On the other side of the street, at 10, av. de l'Échevinage, an Art Deco mansion with a brick and faux stone façade catches our eye (arch. Adolphe Staatje, 1933). The columns that support the awning over the entrance have carved capitals, representing families of penguins, a theme that also appears on the ironwork of the front door. The servant's entrance, in the cellar, is a sign that the occupants were well off.

◀ Mansion, 10, av. de l'Échevinage, arch. A. Staatje

LOUIS HERMAN DE KONINCK (1896-1984)

Louis Herman De Konick, who is widely regarded as one of the key figures of the Modernist movement in Belgium, became one of the pioneers of prefabrication and standardisation because of his research into different materials and building processes, and was an outstanding architect. He mainly built freestanding homes. After graduating from the Academy of Fine Arts in Brussels, he gained a thorough scientific knowledge of the technique of reinforced concrete, following courses at the École industrielle de la Ville de Bruxelles. While the influence of the Viennese Secession is still apparent in his early work, he soon developed his characteristic pure style. In 1928, he introduced the technique of reinforced concrete walls/shells in Belgium. He would spend the rest of his career studying the use of this material. The formal rigour of his designs is the outcome of the constructive logic that concrete imposed, combined with a desire to build affordable housing and control the space, much like Horta did before him. He applied these principles in his lectures at La Cambre from 1942 until 1973. As a member of the Belgian branch of the CIAM, he exhibited the Cubex kitchen, one of the first standardised and juxtaposable kitchen systems, there. Essentially, this was the first fitted kitchen on the market, and it was very successful in Belgium until after the war. Other Uccle projects include his own home (1924) and the studio of the painter Lenglet (1926) at 105 and 103 av. Fond'Roy and the villa of Dr Ley (1934), at 200, av. du Prince d'Orange, which won the Van der Ven prize in 1936.

8/ HOUSE

16, AVENUE DE L'ÉCHEVINAGE, 1180 UCCLE

Architect: Raphaël Delville
Built: 1936

After graduating from the Academy in Brussels, Raphaël Delville (1894-1970), who was the son of the Symbolist painter Jean Deville, trained with Victor Horta, a family friend. He mainly built houses, villas and buildings in a style that evolved from regionalism to Modernism. Pierre-Louis Flouquet praised this design in an article in the journal *Bâtir*[1], emphasising the sunny interior of the house, and the large windows that let the light flow in. He also suggested calling the house "la maison des terrasses" (the house of terraces). He insisted on the fact that this architecture made no concessions in terms of ornamentation, creating its own instead. The façade, with its unique volumetry, was merely the result of a logical and functional layout.
The balconies reveal more about the house's layout. On the first floor, a semi-circular balcony extends the living room, protecting the house's entrance. Its curved awning protects it from sunlight and bad weather. Behind the salon, on the same level as the garden as the parcel was uneven, the architect designed the dining room, the office and the kitchen. The second-floor balcony, which is more intimate, and which is perfectly suited for relaxing, is situated on the same level as the bedrooms. The rooftop terrace, finally, is extremely intimate and can be used for sunbathing. Because of the way the living room extends out, the house is nicely aligned with both of its neighbours. This clearly shows how the architect wanted to incorporate his design among the rest of the houses on this street.

▼ House, 16, av. de l'Échevinage, arch. R. Delville

▼ House, 16, av. de l'Échevinage, floor plan of the first floor. Taken from Bâtir, No. 46, 1936, p. 846

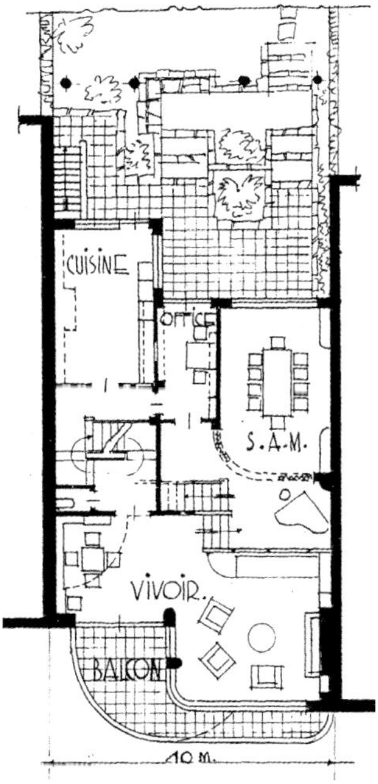

9/ FORMER PRIVATE HOME AND OFFICES

21, AVENUE DE L'ÉCHEVINAGE, 1180 UCCLE

Architect: Léon Sneyers
Built: 1926-1927

Léon Sneyers (1877-1949), a student and associate of Paul Hankar, was influenced by the Viennese Secession which he discovered in 1902, at the International Exhibition of Modern Decorative Arts in Turin. He was passionate about decoration, opening a shop in Brussels, called L'Intérieur moderne, where he sold his own designs as well as those of the *Wiener Werkstätte*. As such, he contributed to the transition from Art Nouveau to Art Deco and the elaboration of the premises of the modernist movement. In 1925, he was asked to design a house on a parcel that was 13 metres wide, for a widow. He must have soon fallen in love with her because the house he built the next year included a large study, which he designed for himself! They were married in November 1930.
The almost austere Art Deco façade, which was inspired by the Viennese Secession, combined brick with faux stone and featured two symmetrical bow-windows as

▼ Former private home and offices of L. Sneyers

well as a monumental porch. The large architect's office on the left of the ground floor extended throughout the house, right up to the garden at the rear. The living room of the architect's private home was situated on the other side of the ground floor, behind the bay windows. A staircase led from the living room to the bedrooms on the first floor. A servant's staircase, meanwhile, connected the rooms at the front right of the house. The reduced height of the windows of the bow-window on the right indicate that these spaces were used by the servants (kitchen on the ground floor, rooms on the upper floors). Sneyers lived in this house until his death. Afterwards, the house's various uses contributed to its degradation. It has since been acquired by a couple of architects, who have restored and renovated it in the spirit of the man who designed it.

At No. 40, a house with red painted frames reminds us of the architectural designs of Antoine Pompe, because of how the architect used brick and combined volumes (arch. Maurice Aerts, 1929-1930).

No.22, avenue Kamerdelle, a well-preserved modernist building. The H. Génicot house, (arch. R. Delville, 1937, listed 13/3/1995), combines hollow and solid volumes, with protruding and recessed elements. The very visible concrete structure is clad with white plaster and filled with bricks. The large bay windows, the ribbon windows and the rooftop terrace once again reveal how important light was in this architect's designs.

◀ House, 40, av. de l'Échevinage, arch. M. Aerts

10/ HAERENS HOUSE

384, AVENUE BRUGMANN AND 2 AVENUE DE LA RAMÉE, 1180 UCCLE

Architect: Antoine Courtens
Built: 1928
Listed: 8/8/1988

This is one of the loveliest examples of Art Deco in Brussels. It was built for the engineer Robert Haerens, who worked as a project manager for the Empain Group, whom Courtens befriended, and his wife Louisa Robelus, a sculptor. The building consisted of two separate dwellings, with separate entrances. The more monumental entrance in avenue Brugmann led to the first-floor apartment of the Haerenses and their daughter, while the entrance in avenue de la Ramée gave access to the ground-floor apartment that they rented out.

Courtens applied Victor Horta's teachings, designing an original façade, which reflects the interior layout of the building, which was adapted to his clients' needs. Until then, architects were happy to do exactly the opposite. The façade's rhythmic composition, the combination of protruding and recessed sections, the geometric decoration and the treatment of the corner rotunda are very similar to the design of the Centre for Fine Arts (arch: V. Horta), of which Courtens also designed a few elements. The geometric patterns on the corner rotunda and on the attic floor also reveal the influence of the American architect Frank Lloyd Wright, whose projects Victor Horta also admired. Courtens, more specifically, was inspired by the *Hollyhock House* in Los Angeles (1917-1920), which used the ornamental motifs of Mayan culture. The intricate wrought ironwork of the two front doors reveal how interested the architect was in this art. In 1928, Courtens became the artistic director of the workshop in Braine-l'Alleud which he employed to produce the ironwork. The apartment of the Haerens, with its ironwork with undulating and stylised motifs, had a central and circular hall, with a dome above it, which allowed natural light to fall into the very heart of the apartment. The hall led to the couple's private quarters as well as the vast reception rooms on the side of avenue Brugmann, which a couple with a busy social life would have needed.

◀ Haerens House

374, avenue Brugmann, a façade with two medallions depicting stylised eagles (arch. J. Hendrickx-Van den Bosch, undated).

At 364-366, the former private home of the architect Jacques Obozinski (1890-1981), which was built in 1921-1922, has a flat, asymmetric façade, which looks rather simple and monumental. This architect, who worked in a modernist style with classical influences, collaborated with Fernand Petit, building several Ostend-Dover ferries and the London-Istanbul car ferry.

▼ Haerens House, entrance in av. Brugmann

▼ Former private home of J. Obozinski, 364-366, av. Brugmann

▼ House, 374, av. Brugmann, arch. Jean Hendrickx-Van den Bosch

11/ CLAIRE MAISON

421, AVENUE BRUGMANN, 1180 UCCLE

Architect: Maurice Houyoux

Built: 1935

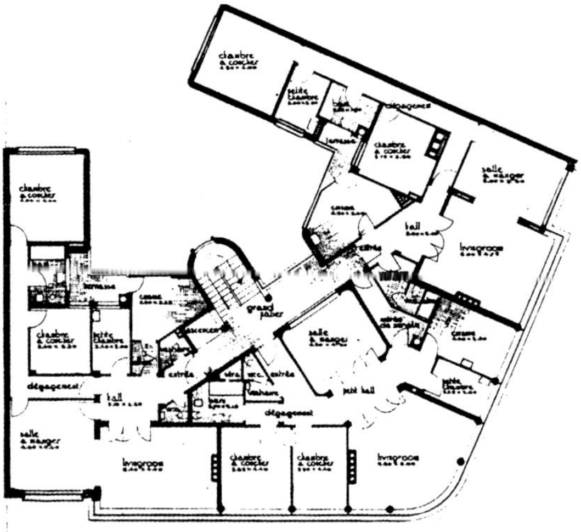

▲ Claire Maison, typical layout of a floor. Taken from Bâtir, No. 42, May 1936, p. 667

After having built factory buildings for the Fabrique nationale de Herstal, Maurice Houyoux (1903-1960) turned to domestic architecture, building several mansions and apartment buildings in Brussels. In 1938, he won the competition for the construction of the Albert I Royal Library. Construction started in the 1950s and ended after the architect's death, in 1969. In this apartment building, Houyoux clearly followed a trend he had already established in his industrial designs: a very simple, almost schematic general layout, with a very clear design. At the time, articles in trade journals stressed that the architect had succeeded in combining art with technique, creating *a very plastic design, with a nice rhythm that was positively drenched in light.*[2]

▼ Claire Maison

▲ House, 124, av. de Boetendael, arch. S. Jasinski

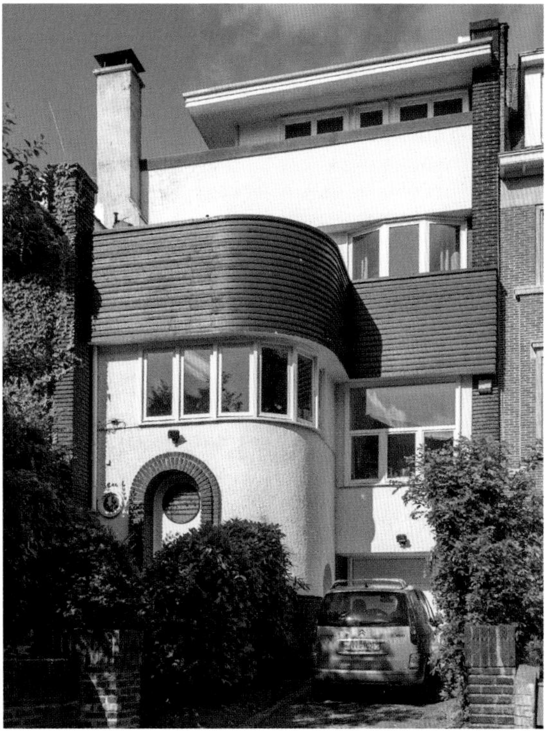

▲ House, 126, av. de Boetendael, arch. L. De Vestel

The ribbon windows, the flat roof, the continuous window sills, the curved corner between the two façades only emphasise the building's horizontal design. The reinforced concrete structure is partly visible through the windows, although most of the window frames have since been replaced. The original window frames, in black-painted metal, contrasted with the white ceramic tiles. The apartment building has three apartments on every floor and two on the ground floor. The preliminary design also included a penthouse, which was never built, however.

124, avenue de Boetendael, a modernist building by Stanislas Jasinski (1931), who built private homes as well as apartment buildings. The façade has very few openings, unlike the south-facing lateral façade, with its many windows through which the light falls in. The overhanging flat roof, the awning over the terraces and the entrance all contribute to the horizontal composition of this façade. The ivy obscures part of the façade, however.

Originally, the façade at No. 126 (1932) stood out because of the contrasting colours and textures with a granular pink coating, the purple facing bricks, the green window frames and the dark wood of the blackened oak shingles. The horizontal wood planks attenuate the verticality of this narrow façade, accentuating the curved balcony. The entrance has a porthole-shaped window and a grate with a musical stave, reminding us that there used to be a music school here! The house was designed by Lucien De Vestel (1902-1967). During the interwar period he practiced a moderate modernist style, after which he concentrated more on technical and building problems. From 1959 until 1967, he designed the plans for the Berlaymont, the European Commission's headquarters.

P
C.D
H

FIFTH WALK

AROUND AVENUE MOLIÈRE

VAN BUUREN MUSEUM TO LA MAISON DE VERRE

This walk, which winds its way around Uccle, Ixelles and even Forest, will allow you to discover housing that was built for the upper middle class. Starting from the van Buuren Museum, we will walk through the elegant Molière and Brugmann neighbourhoods, where we will see designs by such architects as Henry van de Velde, a key figure in modern architecture. The walk ends in front of a Brussels modernist architectural gem, the Maison de Verre or the Glass House.

◂ Mansion, 192, av. Molière, arch. Fr. Van Meulecom

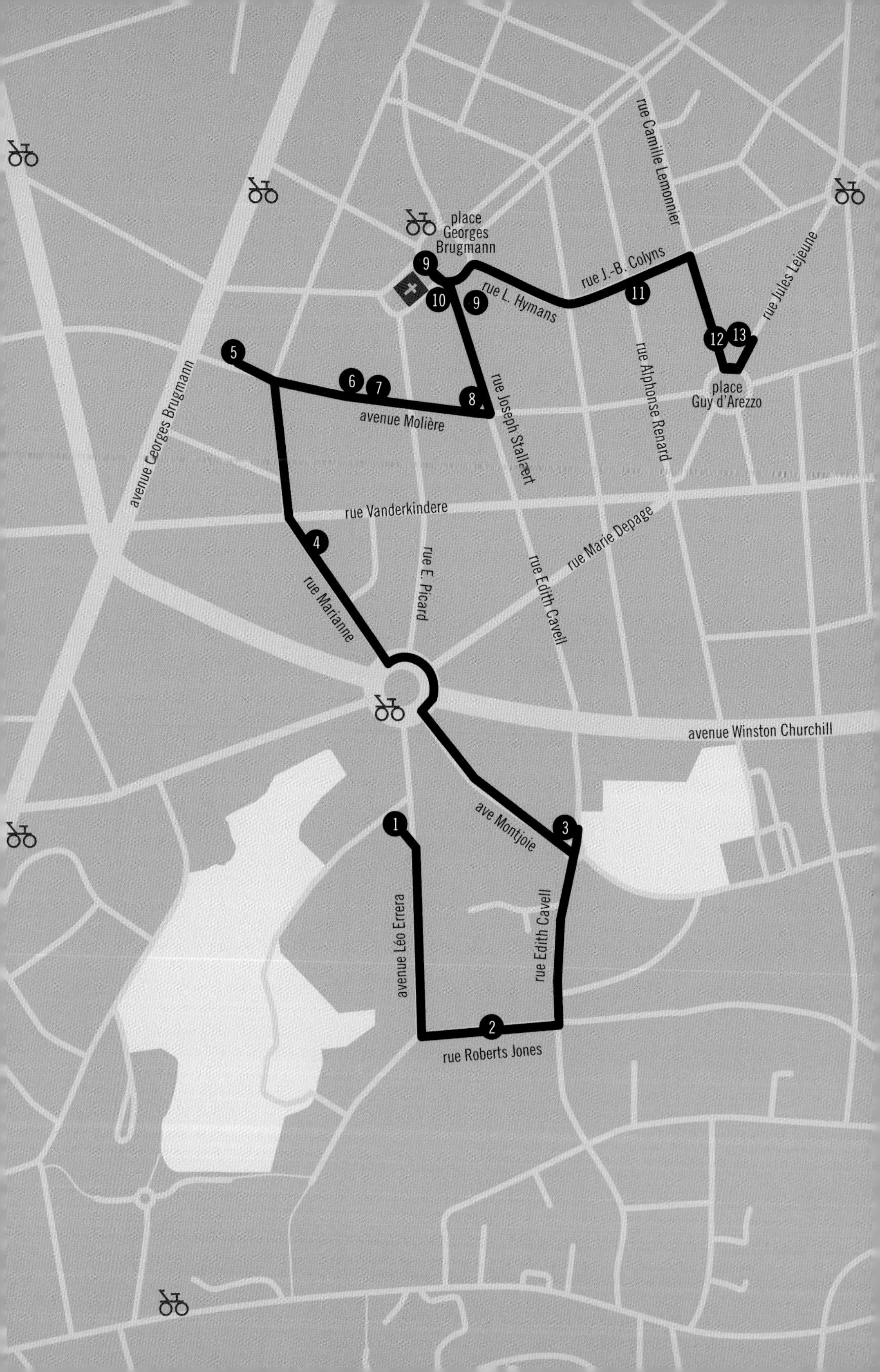

place
Georges
Brugmann
rue Camille Lemonnier
rue J.-B. Colyns
rue L. Hymans
rue Jules Lejeune
place
Guy d'Arezzo
rue Alphonse Renard
rue Joseph Stallaert
avenue Molière
avenue Georges Brugmann
rue Vanderkindere
rue Marie Depage
rue E. Picard
rue Edith Cavell
rue Marianne
avenue Winston Churchill
ave Montjoie
avenue Léo Errera
rue Edith Cavell
rue Roberts Jones
1
2
3
4
5
6
7
8
9
9
10
11
12
13

01 ALICE AND DAVID VAN BUUREN MUSEUM
41, avenue Léo Errera, 1180 Uccle

02 GROUP OF DWELLINGS
28, 30 and 32, rue Roberts Jones, 1180 Uccle

03 GROUP OF DWELLINGS
71-75, rue Edith Cavell and 231-235, avenue Montjoie, 1180 Uccle

04 CHAPEAUX HOUSE
10, rue Marianne, 1180 Uccle

05 MANSION
124, avenue Molière, 1190 Forest

06 MANSION
172, avenue Molière, 1050 Ixelles

07 GHEUDE HOUSE
174, avenue Molière, 1050 Ixelles

08 APARTMENT BUILDING
208-210, avenue Molière, 1050 Ixelles

09 RECTORY AND CHURCH OF OUR LADY OF THE ANNUNCIATION
8-10, rue Joseph Stallaert and place Georges Brugmann, 1050 Ixelles

10 FORMER SURGICAL INSTITUTE OF DR DEPAGE AND FORMER HOSPITAL OF THE BELGIAN RED CROSS
1, rue Joseph Stallaert and 29, place Georges Brugmann, 1050 Ixelles

11 WOLFERS HOUSE
60, rue Alphonse Renard, 1050 Ixelles

12 FORMER PRIVATE HOME AND OFFICES OF THE ARCHITECT
112, rue Camille Lemonnier, 1050 Ixelles

13 MAISON DE VERRE
69, rue Jules Lejeune, 1180 Uccle

1/ ALICE AND DAVID VAN BUUREN MUSEUM

41, AVENUE LÉO ERRERA, 1180 UCCLE

Architects: Léon Emmanuel Govaerts and Alexis Van Vaerenbergh
Built: 1924-1928
Listed: 28/6/2001

A visit to the van Buuren house will allow you to better understand the essence of Art Deco more than any other place. It reflects the discreet and refined personality of its owners and was designed as a gesamtkunstwerk, or a perfect blend of architecture, interior design, collections and gardens. David van Buuren (1886-1955), a Dutchman, moved to Brussels in 1909. His training, his family background and his travels fuelled an interest in the arts, prompting him to take up painting. He made his fortune in banking, however. In 1922, he married a Belgian woman called Alice Piette (1887-1973), with whom he led a refined and elegant life. The couple shared their passion for the arts. Construction on the house started in 1924, while the first garden was completed. The architects Govaerts and Van Vaerenbergh, who worked together on the Vanderborght house, worked closely with David van Buuren on this project. In effect, van Buuren is the real designer of this house and its interior. The house looks both simple and extravagant from the outside. Its architecture is similar to Dutch villas of this era. The use of brick and the brick bonding refer to the Amsterdam School. In 1925, the van Buurens visited the International Exhibition of Modern Decorative and Industrial Arts in Paris, where they chose the designers with whom they would work on the interior design of their house. Nowadays, the entrance hall, the reception rooms, David van Buuren's office and studio are open to the public. The art collection which van Buuren acquired during his lifetime is now exhibited here. He was primarily interested in modern artists, as well as old masters, both Belgian and foreign, buying works by the painters Gustave Van de Woestijne, Constant Permeke... or the sculptors Georges Minne, Jean and Joël Martel... The furniture was designed to measure for each room by Jaap Gidding (Amsterdam School), Studio Dominique (Paris), Joseph Wijnants (Mechelen)... David and Alice van Buuren lived here until their death (barring a short absence during the war years). They received plenty of people, including famous personalities. After the death of her husband, Mrs van Buuren expanded the gardens. She acquired new plots and tasked René Pechère with the construction of a labyrinth and the *Jardin du Cœur* (Heart Garden), which were added to the picturesque garden, which Jules Buyssens created in 1924. In 1970, Alice van Buuren established a foundation, to which she left the property, which reopened as a museum in 1975.

▾ A. and D. van Buuren house, façade seen from the garden

59, avenue Errera, an imposing villa with a large front garden (arch. Adrien Blomme, 1928). Its country aspect is accentuated by the sloping slate roof, with tall chimneys. The conciergerie to the left, with its overhanging flat roof, has a simpler design.

▸ A. and D. van Buuren Museum

▸ A. and D. van Buuren house, cosy corner

2/ GROUP OF DWELLINGS

28, 30 AND 32, RUE ROBERTS JONES, 1180 UCCLE

Architect: Charles Colassin
Built: 1932-1933

Charles Colassin (1893-1942), who admired the Dutch De Stijl movement, had a short career, during which he received several prizes for his designs. In 1934, he won the Van de Ven prize for this group of three modernist houses. The prize was established in 1927 by the industrialist Van de Ven, to promote modern architecture in Belgium. The winning designs attracted due attention in urban planning publications, adding to the renown of its winners. As the plots are positioned at an angle with the street, the architect decided to arrange the houses in a sawtooth pattern. The redents that are thus created allowed him to add corner windows and also emphasised the cubic volumes of the houses.

The architect used similar façade materials to establish a sense of unity between these three houses, with different layouts depending on their usage: brick for the base, coatings on the upper floors. Various changes have since been made, which soften the overall design idea: the houses were repainted, some of the original (metal) window frames and doors were replaced, a floor was added to No. 30. By using reinforced concrete, the architect was able to design a free floor plan. The architect's interior design was equally innovative, with its rational fitted kitchens.

No. 34 (1934-1935), by another architect, is influenced by the positioning of Colassin's houses.

▾ House, 28, rue Roberts Jones

119, rue Edith Cavell, Raphaël Delville (1935) has succeeded in making the most of a very narrow plot. The entrance is on the side, the floors have several horizontal windows. On the street side, the curved balconies and pergola connect beautifully with the adjoining façade.

3/ GROUP OF DWELLINGS
71-75 RUE EDITH CAVELL AND 231-235, AVENUE MONTJOIE, 1180 UCCLE

Architect: Joe Ramaekers
Built: 1929-1930

This group of six modernist dwellings, which was built around an apartment building in the same style (unidentified architect, 1930-1932), was designed for an engineer-entrepreneur who intended to sell them. The cladding and joinery changed over the years, as a result of which the overall idea is no longer that obvious. The triangular projection of the windows on the first two floors adds an original element to the façade, while the upper floors have three small elongated windows. The interiors are rather simple and very similar: the entrance, with a few steps, leads to a hall and stairwell. The family rooms are situated on the first floor while the bedrooms and bathroom are on the second floor. There are three small rooms and a large terrace at the rear on the third floor.

241, avenue Montjoie, a house of which the ornamental Art Deco vocabulary is a typical example of the style of Jean-Baptiste Dewin (1927-1928). He built several houses using qualitative materials including blue stone for the base, brick, white stone and slate for the roof. The horizontality of this façade, which was built on a rather wide plot, is attenuated by the two gables atop the lateral spans.

At No. 196, the former private dwelling and offices (1924-1925) of the architect Joseph Van Neck is an example of the Art Deco style. His offices were on the ground floor, and his studio, with a large skylight, was located under the eaves.

▾ Group of dwellings, 231-235, av. Montjoie, arch. J. Ramaekers

4/ CHAPEAUX HOUSE

10, RUE MARIANNE, 1180 UCCLE

Architect: Victor Bourgeois
Built: 1932

The layout of this modernist house, which was built for an engineer, was very concise. The technical area, with the offices, was situated on the ground floor. The family's day rooms were located on the first floor while the four bedrooms and bathroom were on the second floor. The simple façade protrudes from the first floor onwards and is slightly set back on the level of the second floor terrace. The base is in blue stone, while the rest of the façade is rendered in a clear colour, which contrasted with the dark colour of the window frames and doors (which are now in a light colour).

On the corner of rue Vanderkindere (272) and rue Franz Merjay, a large dwelling stands out because of the pentagonal bow-window on the corner and the combination of horizontal bands of different cladding materials (arch. Robert Puttemans and Émile Poly, 1928).

On the other corner (258-260, rue Vanderkindere), two modest dwellings by Joseph Diongre (1924) are reminiscent of the garden city that the architect had just completed in Molenbeek, called Cité Diongre. The same inspiration, which holds the middle between tradition (with slightly overhanging attic roofs, the use of brick for the base, roofs which originally had red tiles...) and the desire to create a simple design. He has added decorative motifs over the doors, one which features the date of construction, the other a square. Perhaps the square refers to the fact that Diongre was a mason or to his profession as he built the house for himself. The corner house has a balcony with a rounded awning in washed concrete.

◂ Chapeaux house

5/ MANSION
124, AVENUE MOLIÈRE, 1190 FOREST

Architect: Alfred Nyst
Built: 1926

Alfred Nyst (18771972), who initially trained to become an engineer but then changed careers to become an architect, worked for industrial clients initially but he is mainly known for the private homes he built. Originally, he tended towards the Beaux-Arts style, gradually toning down his style, as is obvious in this pre-modernist design with Art Deco influences. The façade features a triangular protruding section, on all the floors, right up to the overhanging cornice. It starts out with an oriel and then evolves into terraces. The right angle is emphasised, on the two first floors, by a stone rib, which has been decorated with mosaics and then extends into a column. The guardrail on the third floor is of masonry, while the one on the third floor is tubular, evidence of the architect's desire to create a lighter, more airy design for the upper floors. On the ground floor, the protruding section rests on a console with the protruding elements that are typical of Art Deco, and which are decorated with colourful mosaics. The window sill of the adjoining window features a black and brown tile design, which is similar to that of the Fournier House (1922, listed in 1995), at 45, square Vergote in Schaerbeek. The carriage entrance is decorated with ironwork with geometric patterns.

◂ Mansion, 124, avenue Molière

6/ MANSION

172, AVENUE MOLIÈRE, 1050 IXELLES

Architect: Jean-Baptiste Dewin
Built: 1910
Listed: 10/10/1996

While this house and the neighbouring house were built before the Great War, they are mentioned here because they herald the architecture of the interwar period.

Jean-Baptiste Dewin (1873-1948) was the son of an ornamentalist sculptor from whom he probably inherited his passion for ornamentation. Over time, he specialised in hospital architecture but he also built several town houses, which evolved from a simple and elegant Art Nouveau style, which was inspired by the work of Paul Hankar and the Viennese Secession, towards an original form of Art Deco with more complex volumes. He also built the town hall of Forest (2, rue du Curé, Forest, 1926-1936, listed: 22/10/1992). The façade of this house still attests to the influence of the Viennese Secession. The symmetric design, around a central oriel, is emphasised by the four pilasters with a finial as a crowning element. The stone façade's elegant decoration combines a series of stylised decorative elements that the architect liked to use, including mosaics, ironwork, stained-glass windows… Some of these elements may discreetly refer to the owner or the architect's membership of the Masonic Lodge. The stylised birds, in profile, on the mosaic panels, refer to the Egyptian god Horus, who was often represented as a falcon with a crown. References to ancient Egypt were very commonplace at the time in the decoration of masonic temples. Horus here might symbolise the sun. The moon is represented at the top of the panel, on the outside. According to the masons, the sun and the moon bring light. Dewin designed every last detail of this gesamtkunstwerk. He also accorded a lot of attention to the floor plan, the quality of the materials and the interior decoration.

◀ Mansion, 172, avenue Molière

7/ GHEUDE HOUSE

174, AVENUE MOLIÈRE, 1050 IXELLES

Architects: Antoine Pompe and Fernand Bodson
Built: 1913

This house has none of the lavish decoration that was so typical of the Art Nouveau style. It was built for a lawyer and reveals how the architects were evolving towards a more rational style. The protruding first-floor oriel is offset by the semi-open space of the entrance and the loggia. While the architects clearly liked using woodwork, they chose not to conceal the metallic lintel on the first floor. The corners of the oriel are decorated with carved masks, an anthropomorphic element that Pompe often used in his designs. The garage was subsequently added. The interior is arranged around a vast stairwell, with plenty of woodwork, which is drenched in light.

25-39 and 46-48, rue Edmond Picard, groups of dwellings built by Fernand Petit in the 1920s (except for 29, in a neo-Elisabethan style, which was the architect's own home and which dates from 1914). They attest to the architect's preference for simple designs and his desire to develop a modern architectural style founded on a classical tradition.

192, avenue Molière, on the corner of rue Picard, an imposing Art Deco mansion (arch. François Van Meulecom, 1928) revealing his appetite for ornamentation with ironwork, stained-glass windows, fruit baskets in the bas-reliefs, the combination of red brick with faux white stone elements... The main entrance was in avenue Molière while the servant's entrance was in rue Picard.

◂ Gheude House

ANTOINE POMPE (1873-1980)

Antoine Pompe, who was largely self-taught, studied drawing and applied art in Brussels and in Germany. After work placements and thanks to various professional experiences, Pompe learnt more about a variety of techniques such as metal engraving, ironwork, drawing, the creation of furniture and flatware, jewellery, joinery... and finally architecture! Working with an architect called Lener, Pompe built the Palace Hotel, in place Rogier, in 1908. At the age of 37, in 1910, he built his first own project: the clinic of Dr Van Neck, at 53, rue Wafelaerts, in Saint-Gilles (listed: 7/12/1981, see p. 13), which is a manifesto of rationalist architecture. From 1910 until 1921, Pompe worked with his associate Fernand Bodson on various projects, which combined an ideological commitment with formal and technological inventions, helping to rebuild the country after the war and building garden cities. After he failed to secure public contracts, Pompe essentially designed villas and small apartment buildings. Although the design is rationalist, they also point to the architect's interest in a human and emotional approach to architecture. Pompe liked to combine brick with wood, often creating buildings with picturesque volumes, the interiors of which bathed in a soft light. Pompe, who only became an architect later in life, had a long career as he lived to the ripe old age of 106! A man with great fantasy, who was capable of doing a lot with very little, he had plenty of verve and was not afraid of expressing his opinion in contentious articles. A tireless inventor, he had several patents in construction and carpentry. He even designed a revolutionary roller-skate.

8/ APARTMENT BUILDING

208-210, AVENUE MOLIÈRE, 1050 IXELLES

Architect: Joe Ramaekers
Built: 1928-1930
Listed: 16/3/1995

Joe Ramaekers (1900-1975) is mainly known for the various buildings and homes he built in Brussels around the 1930s. Using large sections of dark brick, combined with expressive and evocative designs, his projects are clearly influenced by the Amsterdam School. This modernist building is probably one of his best. The floor plans of the apartments vary, indicating that some were sold on spec, even before they were completed.

The mauve, Belvédère-type brick façades are defined by the two groups of protruding spans which protrude from the building and which have been laid out on either side of the polygonal corner tower. The top of it is emphasised by bands of bricks, which are slightly recessed. Originally, the wood frames were painted dark green and edged with gold. The building's entrance, in avenue Molière, has a service entrance, which leads to the concierge's office and an entrance to the ground floor apartment. The shared spaces are well designed, with interesting contrasts in colour and material. The architect clearly sought to achieve symmetry and liked geometric patterns. The walls are covered with light ceramic tiles, with bands of black ceramic tiles here and there. The lustre of the tiles contrasts with the mat dark brick elements. The ceiling lights, which have various shapes, the stained-glass windows with geometric shapes, add luminous colourful accents to the spaces.

269-271, Avenue Molière is easy to recognise, with its two Art Deco façades by Jean-Baptiste Dewin (1922-1923), which feature ironwork with lavish ornamentation with plant and animal motifs, carved stone, stained-glass windows...

◄ Apartment building, 208-210, av. Molière

9/ RECTORY AND CHURCH OF OUR LADY OF THE ANNUNCIATION

8-10, RUE JOSEPH STALLAERT AND PLACE GEORGES BRUGMANN, 1050 IXELLES

Architect: Camille Damman
Built: 1925 and 1932-1934

As it took longer than expected to build the Church of the Annunciation, even though it was already featured in the land development plans for the neighbourhood, which date from 1898, a provisional church was built in 1916 at 6, rue Joseph Stallaert. Nowadays it is used as a parish community centre (Le Fanal). Next to it, Camille Damman built the rectory of the future church. The brick façade of the rectory features white stone elements with stylised floral motifs. The façades have several windows, with different shapes, which have been aligned according to a very specific rhythm. They all still have the original window frames. The multiple divisions of the windows combine to create a central square with a small stained-glass window in it. The side entrance, with its covered porch, the windows and doors of which still have the original ironwork and windows, leads to the priest's apartments. The streetside entrance, with its awning with floral motifs, led to the upper floors, where the vicars' apartments were situated. They have since been renovated and are now rented out.

The project also included a theatre (part of the community centre) at 12, rue Stallaert. This amenity, which has since been renovated, is now used by youth movements. The Church of the Annunciation, which dates from 1932-1934, is built in a neo-Roman style, with Art Deco additions and stands out because of its brick masonry. The architect emphasised the contrasts between materials in various colours, both in the interior and on the exterior of the building, using brown brick and white stone, dark and light marble for the confessionals, stained-glass windows, floor tiles in bright colours with a geometric pattern.

12-20, Place Brugmann and 128-132, rue Berkendael, behind the church, a group of apartment buildings (arch. Paul Picquet, 1928-1929) with very simple rendered façades, with openwork concrete balconies, covered terraces on the fifth floor that protrude from the façade and a dome on the corner.

▼ Rectory, 8-10, rue J. Stallaert

▶ Notre-Dame de l'Annonciation / Church of Our Lady of the Annunciation, pl. Brugmann

▶ Apartment building, 12-20, pl. Brugmann and 128-132, rue Berkendael, arch. P. Picquet

10/ FORMER SURGICAL INSTITUTE OF DR DEPAGE AND FORMER HOSPITAL OF THE BELGIAN RED CROSS

1, RUE JOSEPH STALLAERT AND 29, PLACE GEORGES BRUGMANN, 1050 IXELLES

Architect: Jean-Baptiste Dewin
Built: 1905 and 1926
Listed: 18/12/2003

In 1903, Dr Depage asked Jean-Baptiste Dewin to build him a private clinic. Its style is still very reminiscent of the geometric Art Nouveau trend, which was influenced by the Viennese Secession. He designed the central building, which gives out onto place Brugmann. In 1926, Dewin was tasked with extending the clinic, which by then was the property of the Belgian Red Cross. He built a new, much simpler building on the corner of the square and rue Stallaert. Originally there were small red tiles in the window frames, which traced a Red Cross. The corner monument, which was created with the sculptor Godefroid Devreese, pays tribute to Dr Depage (1862-1925), a key figure in the early twentieth-century Belgian surgical profession, whose contribution to the organisation of hospital care was significant. Among others, he founded the first Belgian nursing school. During World War I, he was tasked with the organisation of the army's health services. He also set up several hospitals near combat zones. Afterwards the hospital building was enlarged by other architects. The building attests to the evolution in medical architecture from 1904 until 1964. After its decommissioning, only the Dewin buildings were preserved and incorporated in a new luxury real estate project. A bit further abreast, on the corner of rue Edit Cavell and rue Marie Depage, Dewin also built the buildings of the Belgian Nursing School, which Edith Cavell managed before World War I. These buildings are now longer as the complex was expanded several times to become the Edith Cavell Hospital.

◂ Former surgical institute of Dr Depage, building dating from 1905, 29, pl. G. Brugmann

▲ Former Red Cross building, extension of 1926, 1, rue J. Stallaert

◀ Apartment and office building, 9-9c, rue L. Hymans, arch. A. Darche

Rue Louis Hymans 9-9C, an apartment and office building (arch. André Darche, 1928), for which you need to step back to take it in. The design of this three-floor building is quite original. By progressively moving back the lateral façade, the architect has succeeded in creating a series of right angles, and room for a garden. Yellow and violet bricks adorn the façades, emphasising certain volumes. The white stone on the corners accentuates the Expressionist design of this building, which was influenced by the Amsterdam School, even more. The left door (9C) leads to the apartments, with one on every floor, from the second floor upwards. The main entrance (9B) led to the architect's offices and studio on the ground floor. The right door, next to the carriage entrance, is extended with a gallery leading to the private entrance of the large first-floor apartment, where the architect once lived.

11/ WOLFERS HOUSE

60, RUE ALPHONSE RENARD, 1050 IXELLES

Architect: Henry van de Velde
Built: 1930-1931
Listed: 4/10/1983

This house, which is a good example of Henry van de Velde's second Belgian period, was commissioned in 1929 by Raymond Wolfers, the father of the jeweller Philippe Wolfers. In the Seventies, it was almost demolished. In 1983, it was listed and restored. As the house is built on a rather irregular corner plot, the architect decided to incorporate the entrance in the rear façade. You reach the entrance through a metal gate, while a second gate, at the end of the garden, leads to the garage. The yellow brick façade, with its flat roof, has been kept extremely simple. Its horizontal appearance is emphasised by the elongated, rounded brick the architect chose to use on the corners and on the accentuated horizontal joints, the alignment of the windows and a small awning over the second-floor windows in rue Renard. The design is not cluttered by a gutter or a drainpipe. The floor plan was influenced by the shape of the plot on which the house was built. The light-drenched ground floor is occupied by the reception areas. The black marble, which is used throughout, accentuates the simplicity of the rooms. On the ground floor, an exterior staircase leads from the kitchen directly into the garden. The first floor is reserved for the bedrooms of the masters of the house while the second floor has rooms for the servants and a gym. Every floor has a large terrace, which is set back and positioned over the entrance.

▼ Maison Wolfers

HENRY VAN DE VELDE (1863-1957)

Henry van de Velde, a man who was known for the multiplicity of his talents and a European before the term was even coined, is one of the figureheads of twentieth-century art history. A renowned painter, he soon turned to the decorative arts, deciding to design beautiful and practical everyday objects, that could also be reproduced. In 1895, he created his first architectural design, building Bloemenwerf, his home in Uccle. Its rational design was a clear manifestation of his desire to reject any ornament that was inspired by the styles of the past. He soon received many more commissions for interior designs, prompting him to establish his own manufacturing company in 1899. In 1900, he moved to Berlin, after which he was named artistic adviser to the Grand Duke of Saxony-Weimar in 1902, who tasked him with the revival of the region's art industries. Between 1904 and 1911, he established the School of Fine Arts in Weimar and his own school of decorative arts (which was later named Bauhaus in 1919). The programme was based on the immediate cultivation of the student's sensibility to beauty, rather than the study of styles.

During the wartime years, he fled to Switzerland, moving to the Netherlands in 1919 at the behest of two of his patrons, the Kröller-Müllers. In 1926, he returned to Belgium where he founded and directed the Higher Institute of Decorative Arts La Cambre and where he became one of the key figures of the Belgian architectural avant-garde. During this period, he built several private dwellings and the library of Ghent University (1933-1942), based on a rationalist aesthetic. He was also appointed artistic adviser of the National Society of Belgian Railways, oversaw the construction of the Belgian pavilions of the World Fairs in Paris in 1937 and New York in 1939. Under the Germans, he was appointed aesthetic adviser to the General Commissariat for the country's reconstruction. He was prosecuted for this after the war, but the case was dismissed. He subsequently moved to Switzerland where he devoted himself to writing his memoirs.

12/ FORMER PRIVATE HOME AND OFFICES OF THE ARCHITECT

112, RUE CAMILLE LEMONNIER, 1050 IXELLES

Architect: Robert Puttemans
Built: 1929

Robert Puttemans (1902-1978) used restraint and simplicity in his first designs, for private homes and small apartment buildings. After the stock market crash of 1929, he went to work for his former lecturer, Joseph Van Neck, as the head of office for the 1935 World Fair. Subsequently, he focused on rather complex buildings such as schools, hospitals, exhibition pavilions, designing them alone or in association with other architects. He also lectured for many years at the ULB and La Cambre.

This purposefully simple asymmetric brick façade was clearly designed for an office building on the ground floor with a private dwelling above it. On the first floor, light flows in through the large window of the former studio with its high ceiling. The rest of the floor consists of the kitchen, living and dining room. On the second floor, where the bedrooms are located, an exterior staircase leads to the vast rooftop garden, which was added for practical reasons. The idea was to *eliminate the dusty attics and use the reclaimed space for the occupants, creating a well-exposed outdoor area, with a free and simple design, catering to the needs of modern urban dwellers. Here they could breathe in fresh air, sunbathe, exercise, relax, play games, etc.*[1]

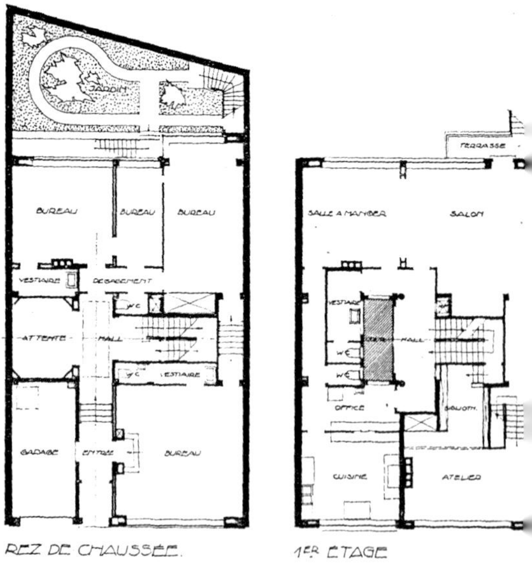

▲ Floor plan of two floors. Taken from La Cité, No. 3, 1931

◀ Former private home and offices of Robert Puttemans

13/ MAISON DE VERRE / GLASS HOUSE

69, RUE JULES LEJEUNE, 1180 UCCLE

Architect: Paul-Amaury Michel
Built: 1935-1936
Listed: 24/9/1998

Paul-Amaury Michel (1912–1988) belongs to the first generation of architects that was educated at Le Cambre, where he befriended Henry van de Velde. During his studies, he discovered the avant-garde buildings of Belgium. After his graduation, in 1934, he travelled to the Netherlands and France, where he met Robert Mallet-Stevens, Pierre Chareau and Le Corbusier. La Maison de Verre, or the Glass House, his first design and own home, earned him the recognition of his fellow modernist architects, as well as plenty of praise from architectural journals and his first nomination for the Van de Ven Prize (1937). He was invited to join the CIAM from 1936.

This design pays tribute to a dwelling of the same name, built by Pierre Chareau in Paris, in 1928-1931, for Dr Dalsace. The latter has a glass façade that gives out onto a courtyard. While the plot was very narrow, it had one advantage, namely that the building to the left only had one floor and was slightly set back from the street. As a result, the architect was able to design a building with a certain volume, in perspective, rather than simply insert a façade between two buildings. He applied Le Corbusier's *Five Points of Architecture* (1927) in this rational design, which is stripped of any ornamentation, i.e., part of the structure rests on pilotis (a free-standing corner

▼ Maison de Verre, main façade

▼ Maison de Verre, rear façade

column on the ground floor), a rooftop terrace, an open ground plan and a façade free from structural constraints. On the ground floor, you can see the small garden through the passage under the house. It also protects visitors from the elements. The rest of this floor is occupied by the entrance hall and a kitchen with Cubex furniture. The relatively narrow main staircase leads to the upper floors. The first two floors consist of a duplex, with a tall window in the façade. The lower level comprises the dining room and a living room on the street side. The bedroom and bathroom are on the upper level, on the garden side. At the front of the building, the library and the corner study form a gallery above the living room. On the third floor, three small rooms make up the rear, while a rooftop terrace and solarium have been fitted with a concrete dining table. The rear façade is the most original element of this design. The architect designed a wall, made of translucent glass blocks, combined with horizontal tilting windows with clear glass, to allow the light to fall into the rooms while protecting the privacy of the house's occupants. The house, which was sold in 1942, underwent renovations and alterations and its concrete structure gradually deteriorated. It remained vacant for many years until it was bought in 1997 by a private individual who filed an application to have the building listed and entrusted Bernard Baines and Christian Gilot with the restoration. They attempted to preserve as many of the original elements as possible but the rear façade, which was too damaged, had to be rebuilt from scratch, identical to the original. Paul-Amaury Michel was arrested and deported to the concentration camps in 1943 but succeeded in escaping in 1945. From 1946 onwards, he went back to work, building numerous residential, commercial and industrial buildings as well as villas. From 1950, he turned to the International Style, building exhibition pavilions and booths in Europe and Africa.

Avenue Molière 292, the Clarté Building (arch. P.-A. Michel, 1939-1941) is a tribute to Le Corbusier, who built a building with the same name in Geneva (1931-1932). Here light defines the architecture, as the layout has been conceived in such a way that there is daylight in every room. The building was awarded the Van de Ven prize in 1939 for its white walls, the absence of any decoration whatsoever and its volumes.

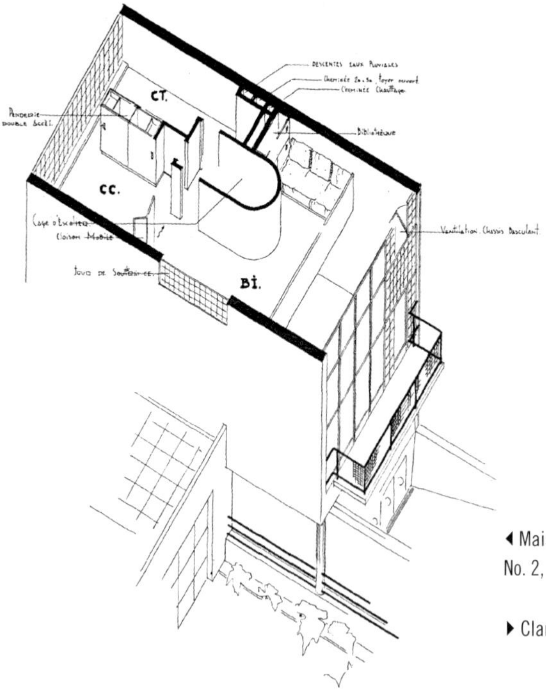

◂ Maison de Verre / Glass house, axonometry. Taken from L'Époque, No. 2, 1937, p. 402

▸ Clarté Building, av. Molière 292

SIXTH WALK

WEST OF BRUSSELS

ST JOHN THE BAPTIST AT THE BÉGUINAGE TO TOUR AND TAXIS

No publication on the architecture of the interwar period in Brussels would be complete without a chapter on social housing and the architecture on the other side of the canal. This route allows us to combine the two. Be aware that this is a long route, which is more suited for a bike tour. We explore Molenbeek-Saint-Jean, where urban and industrial development were closely interlinked, following the extension of the canal to Charleroi in 1832. Nicknamed Little Manchester because of the large number of small industries, the municipality drew a large working-class population, which lived in crowded homes, which lacked the mod cons and hygiene. After World War I, the authorities finally started to develop a social housing policy. The west of Molenbeek, on the other side of the railway which cuts through the municipality, as well as the municipalities of Jette, Berchem-Sainte-Agathe, Ganshoren and part of Koekelberg mainly developed during the interwar period. In those days, housing consisted of small working-class or upper middle-class houses or garden cities. This route also includes one of the largest Art Deco buildings that was ever built: the Basilica of Koekelberg.

◂ Interior view of the cupola of the national Basilica of the Sacred Heart, esplanade of the basilica

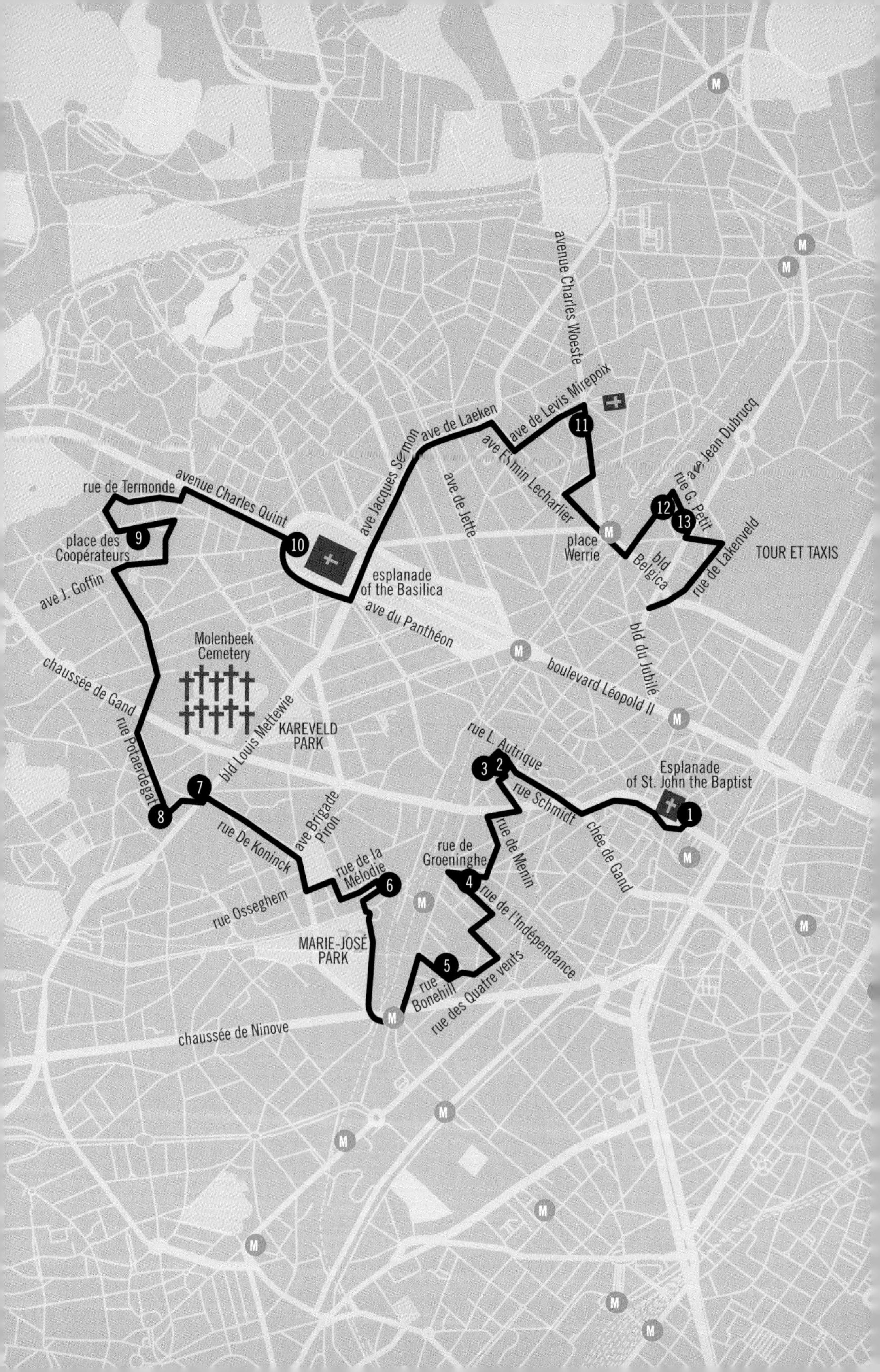

avenue Charles Woeste
ave de Levis Mirepoix
ave de Laeken
ave Jacques Sermon
ave Firmin Lecharlier
ave de Jette
ave Jean Dubrucq
rue G. Petit
rue de Termonde
avenue Charles Quint
place des Coopérateurs
ave J. Goffin
esplanade of the Basilica
ave du Panthéon
place Werrie
bld Belgica
rue de Lakenveld
TOUR ET TAXIS
Molenbeek Cemetery
chaussée de Gand
rue Potaerdegat
bld Louis Mettewie
KAREVELD PARK
boulevard Léopold II
bld du Jubilé
rue L. Autrique
Esplanade of St. John the Baptist
rue Schmidt
chée de Gand
rue De Koninck
ave Brigade Piron
rue de la Mélodie
rue de Groeninghe
rue de Menin
rue de l'Indépendance
rue Osseghem
MARIE-JOSÉ PARK
rue Bonehill
rue des Quatre vents
chaussée de Ninove

01 CHURCH OF ST JOHN THE BAPTIST
parvis Saint-Jean-Baptiste, 1080 Molenbeek-Saint-Jean

02 LOGEMENTS DU FOYER KOEKELBERGEOIS
rue Léon Autrique, rue Stepman and rue du Cubisme, 1081 Koekelberg

03 BOVENHUIS APARTMENT BUILDING
11-21, rue du Cubisme, 1081 Koekelberg

04 CITÉ VAN HEMELRIJCK
between rue de l'Indépendance (131) and rue de Groeninghe, 1080 Molenbeek-Saint-Jean

05 COUR SAINT-LAZARE
31-109, rue Edmond Bonehill and 1-119, rue Louis De Gunst, 1080 Molenbeek-Saint-Jean

06 GROUP OF DWELLINGS
rue de la Mélodie, rue de l'Accord and rue Eugène Degorge and place du Chant d'Alouette, 1080 Molenbeek-Saint-Jean

07 CITÉ DIONGRE
rue des Béguines, rue de Bruges and Joseph Diongre, 1080 Molenbeek-Saint-Jean

08 CITÉ DE SAULNIER
rue Potaerdegat and rue des Béguines and avenue Armand de Saulnier, 1080 Molenbeek-Saint-Jean

09 CITÉ MODERNE
place des Coopérateurs and surrounding area, 1082 Berchem-Sainte-Agathe

10 NATIONAL BASILICA OF THE SACRED HEART
1, parvis de la Basilique, 1083 Ganshoren and 1081 Koekelberg

11 WITHUIS
183, avenue Charles Woeste, 1090 Jette

12 CITÉ DUBRUCQ
184-198, avenue Jean Dubrucq, 1080 Molenbeek-Saint-Jean

13 ANCIENS ÉTABLISSEMENTS GOSSET
6, rue Gabrielle Petit, 1080 Molenbeek-Saint-Jean

1/ CHURCH OF ST JOHN THE BAPTIST

PARVIS SAINT-JEAN-BAPTISTE, 1080 MOLENBEEK-SAINT-JEAN

Architect: Joseph Diongre
Built: 1931-1932
Listed: 29/2/1984

In 1930, the municipal authorities entrusted Joseph Diongre, who had already designed several social housing projects for Le Logement Molenbeekois, with a new project, asking him to build a new church to replace the old one, which had become too small. As he only had a limited budget to work with, the architect built a reinforced concrete building, with six parabolic arches, which were also visible inside the building, and which made the nave look lighter and bigger. He was inspired by the projects of the French engineer Freyssinet, who built the concrete arches for the Orly aerodrome, and by the French architect Auguste Perret, who built a reinforced concrete church in Le Raincy in 1922-1923. On the outside, the structure is composed of massive, stepped volumes. The lower elements are just as high as the lateral naves. While the architect used the traditional Latin-cross plan, he decided to incorporate the 56-metre tall bell tower in the façade. The concrete was concealed from view. The exterior walls were clad with slabs of Brauvilliers stone (France) while the walls and the bases of the parabolic arches inside the church were covered with marble panels. Elsewhere, the concrete was hidden under a layer of rough plaster. The façade has a large Latin-cross opening with a stained-glass window that was produced by the master glassmaker Crickx. The colourful glass is set in concrete frames. It features bas-reliefs, including the baptism of Christ and smaller emblems of the four Evangelists. The tower, the lateral façades and the roof all have several glazed openings, letting plenty of light into the building. Over time, the church has deteriorated substantially. A renovation was undertaken by Arsis, from 1998 until 2010.

◀ Saint John the Baptist

2/ LOGEMENTS DU FOYER KOEKELBERGEOIS
RUE LÉON AUTRIQUE, RUE STEPMAN AND RUE DU CUBISME, 1081 KOEKELBERG

Built: 1921-1922

This group of apartment buildings was commissioned by Le Foyer Koekelbergeois, the local social housing authority. Various architects worked on the project, including Arthur Pladet (21, rue Autrique and 22, rue du Cubisme), Albert de Valeriola (23-25, rue Autrique and 26-24, rue du Cubisme) and Fernand Brunfaut (6-10, rue Stepman). The triangular ground-floor windows of the Pladet buildings jut out from the building. A carved panel on top of the entrances lists the building's name, Le Foyer Victoria. Although these buildings were owned by Foyer Koekelbergeois, they were built at the behest of the director of the Victoria chocolate/biscuit factory, who also happened to be the mayor of the municipality. The idea was to build housing for the factory workers. The semi-circular arches of the entrances of the Valeriola buildings are decorated in different ways. The keystones feature women's faces with floral motifs around them, while the jambs depict two eagles in profile, with the letters F and K for Le Foyer Koekelbergeois.

▸ Detail of a building by A. Pladet, social housing of Le Foyer Koekelbergeois

▾ Social housing of Le Foyer Koekelbergeois, corner of rue Autrique and rue Stepman

SOCIAL HOUSING

The history of social housing is rife with choices, clashes between different models, tensions between proponents of the development of low-cost rental housing and proponents of a policy to promote home ownership. At the end of the nineteenth century, the industrial boom in Brussels attracted many families, who settled near the factories or businesses where they worked, in a rather anarchic manner. The housing situation of workers was catastrophic: sordid slums, a lack of space and hygiene, intolerable promiscuity... The Law of 1889 made it possible for workers who were financially better off to buy a home and was a first attempt to find a solution. This law paved the way for the establishment of parapublic housing authorities, for the construction, purchase, sale or rental of housing for the working classes. The Cité Hellemans (1912) was built around this time for example, consisting of multi-family buildings, that replaced slums. After the Great War, the housing shortage forced the authorities to adopt a socialist law in 1919, which established the National Society of Affordable Houses and Housing (Société nationale des Habitations et Logements à Bon Marché, SNHLBM). It was an umbrella organisation for the existing local parapublic housing authorities, which aimed to promote the establishment of new authorities and finance the construction of housing. In the early Twenties, this impetus led to the construction of garden cities. These single-family housing estates were built in green surroundings, on the city's fringe. At the same time, apartment buildings with multiple floors were built in urban areas. This type of building ended up being the winning solution as it cost less and met the requirements of the largest number. These dwellings usually consisted of a living area, one to three bedrooms, a laundry room which was used as a kitchen, for the laundry and for washing oneself and a small terrace that led to a WC.

3/ BOVENHUIS APARTMENT BUILDING

11-21, RUE DU CUBISME, 1081 KOEKELBERG

Architect: Victor Bourgeois
Built: 1922

This small building, which was built for the tenants' association of La Cité Moderne, has a rather complex layout, which contrasts with the façade's relatively simple appearance. Drawing inspiration from Dutch projects, most of Bourgeois's apartments have a front door that gives out onto the street. Hence the name *Bovenhuis*, which can be translated as "house on an upper floor". Only four of the twelve apartments share a front door. The others are duplex apartments, on the first two floors, or are all on one level, on the second floor. There was a shop on the corner, with a house behind it. The composition of the windows, the front doors and the brick façades, with horizontal and vertical projections, points to the influence of De Stijl and Piet Mondrian's paintings. The lintels, the thresholds and the awnings are in washed concrete. The apartments are scheduled to be renovated. The street owes its name to this building, which is a Brussels manifesto of Cubism in architecture.

Up the street, on the corner of rue J. Jacquet and rue A. Court, a large group of apartment buildings around an inner courtyard was built by the Foyer Koekelbergeois in 1921, shortly after it was founded. It includes projects by F. Brunfaut (14-18, rue J. Jacquet), V. Bourgeois (1-3, rue A. Court), A. de Valeriola (5-7, rue A. Court) and A. Pladet (9, rue A. Court).

Washed concrete is a type of concrete that is achieved by washing the top layer off the concrete with a high-pressure water jet, exposing the granular surface below. It requires almost no maintenance.

VICTOR BOURGEOIS (1897-1962)

This architect was one of the most active and best-known proponents of the modernist movement in Belgium. He rejected the historicism that was taught at the academy, founding two journals with his brother Pierre Bourgeois, called *Au Volant* (1919) and *Le Geste* (1919-1920). In them, they proclaimed their desire to build a society on entirely new foundations and principles. In 1922, the Bourgeois brothers founded the weekly magazine *7 Arts* (1922-1928), which built bridges between the various international avant-garde movements and the core of the modernist movement in Belgium. In the early Twenties, Bourgeois briefly collaborated with the SNHLBM, and travelled to the Netherlands where he discovered the work of the De Stijl movement. Its influence is apparent in his early projects. He became famous following the construction of the Cité Moderne (1922-1925), which allowed him to play a key role in the organisation of the CIAM. The third conference was held in Brussels in 1930 at his suggestion. By the end of the Twenties, he focused on smaller commissions, building houses and villas. The references to De Stijl gradually disappeared, making way for a more formal research, combining a pure vocabulary that was inspired by Le Corbusier and robust volumes with rounded corners and cylindrical shapes. In the Thirties, he worked on regional planning projects, presenting an urban planning project for *Nouveau Bruxelles*, suggesting that enormous buildings be constructed as a solution to the housing shortage. His many functionalist buildings include exhibition pavilions, community centres, schools, buildings for the health sector, industry or the public authorities. He spent many years teaching at La Cambre and made a lasting impression on the generation of post-war architects.

◀ Home and studio of the sculptor Oscar Jespers, 149, av. Du Prince Héritier, Woluwe-Saint-Lambert, arch. V. Bourgeois, 1928

4/ CITÉ VAN HEMELRIJCK

BETWEEN RUE DE L'INDÉPENDANCE (131) AND RUE DE GROENINGHE, 1080 MOLENBEEK-SAINT-JEAN

Architect: Joseph Diongre
Built: 1932-1933

Le Logement Molenbeekois started building housing relatively late in this already very populated neighbourhood. The housing authority was established in 1899. Initially, it was easier and less costly to build on unbuilt parcels that were further away from the municipality's centre, rather than clearing the densely-populated neighbourhoods. The housing crisis of the interwar period forced society to rethink its strategy and policy. Gradually, the authorities started to build in the neighbourhood, taking advantage of parcels and resources that became available. Cité Van Hemelrijck was built in this context, for people who were evicted from slums or unsanitary housing. The adjoining courtyards of the two buildings are connected by a stairwell – which now also has a lift – which leads to the passageways and the apartments. The contrast between the brick façades on the street side, with rows of bow-windows, and the reinforced concrete façades on the courtyard side couldn't be greater. The locals called this building block *the block of thieves*, because the building resembled a prison. It was recently renovated.

◂ Cité Van Hemelrijck

5/ COUR SAINT-LAZARE

31-109, RUE EDMOND BONEHILL AND 1-119, RUE LOUIS DE GUNST, 1080 MOLENBEEK-SAINT-JEAN

Architect: Joseph Diongre
Built: 1926-1927

In 1926, Diongre was asked by Le Logement Molenbeekois to build a housing estate in a very short time frame, which could house dozens of families who lived in slums. The parcel was both close to the municipality's centre and the more industrial neighbourhood around West Station. He designed a modernist group of buildings, in reinforced concrete, with 180 units in five wings on five levels. Two wings form the corner of rue Bonehill and rue De Gunst, while the other three wings form a U shape within the building block, around a courtyard. The ground floor apartments give out directly onto the street or the courtyard. The apartments on the upper floors all give out onto passageways, with wide stairwells. The apartments offered rudimentary comfort but were a much better option than the slums where the inhabitants formerly lived. The layout was very rational. The front door opened out into the living room. The apartment also had two bedrooms, a laundry room and a WC on a small terrace at the rear. In 2012, the building was deemed no longer to meet building standards, which is why it was thoroughly renovated. After the renovation, the site will have 84 apartments and its former structure will have been restored. The architects have paid special attention to the passageways for example, which lend the building its unique appearance. The passageways contributed to the special ambience in the cité.[1] The proximity between the inhabitants sometimes was a source of arguments. At the same time, it also fostered a great sense of solidarity. In the summer, people would sit in the passages, chatting with each other, like in the villages or in the slums.

6/ HOUSING ESTATE

RUE DE LA MÉLODIE, RUE DE L'ACCORD AND RUE EUGÈNE DEGORGE AND PLACE DU CHANT D'ALOUETTE, 1080 MOLENBEEK-SAINT-JEAN

Architect: François Van Meulecom
Built: 1938

After crossing the railway tracks, near West Station, we find ourselves in a neighbourhood that vividly illustrates a chapter in the history of affordable housing since the end of the nineteenth century right up to the end of World War II. The housing includes individual houses to buy or rent as well as apartment buildings and a low-rise school that was built in 1935.

On the corner of rue de la Mélodie and place du Chant de l'Alouette and the adjoining streets, 32 dwellings, which were designed by François Van Meulecom, stand out because of the small porthole-shaped window on the upper floor. They were built on a shoestring budget but still look slightly bourgeois. The authorities hoped that they would attract a more well-off population to the neighbourhood by selling off these houses. Their layout shows the extent to which cheap housing had come to mean more mod cons.

On the ground floor, a hallway led to the other rooms. You no longer entered the house through the living room, like in working-class accommodation. On the first floor, the houses also had a bathroom. These houses were sold just before World War II broke out.

The two apartment buildings at 34-36, rue Demessemaeker were built by Van Meulecom in 1932-34 for Le Logement Molenbeekois. The glazed spans above the entrance draw daylight into the stairwells. A large entrance, with the inscription Cité Van Meulecom above it, leads to the inside of the building block and the low-income houses that were built for elderly residents (arch. F. Van Meulecom, 1924). This brick façades, which are painted wide, and which features triangular pediments and doors with porthole-shaped windows, are similar to the other buildings.

The corner of rue du Lierre (28) and rue Demessemaeker (33-35) is occupied by an apartment building by Van Meulecom that dates from 1922. Rue du Gulden bodem and rue Ostendael are lined with individual dwellings, which were built by the architect Armand de Saulnier between 1925 and 1928 for Le Logement Molenbeekois. The houses were subsequently sold. The corner buildings still belong to the housing authority. The ground floor premises were designed to accommodate shops.

▾ Access to Cité Van Meulecom, rue Demessemaeker, arch. Fr. Van Meulecom

▾ Dwellings, 6 and 8, rue de l'Accord, arch. Fr. Van Meulecom

7/ CITÉ DIONGRE

RUE DES BÉGUINES, RUE DE BRUGES AND RUE JOSEPH DIONGRE, 1080 MOLENBEEK-SAINT-JEAN

Architect: Joseph Diongre
Built: 1924-1925

In 1921, Le Logement Molenbeekois acquired a property with the idea of building a garden city there. The housing authority wanted to build high-quality urban neighbourhoods, in addition to the tower blocks that were being constructed in densely-populated neighbourhoods to cater to pressing needs. At the time, boulevard Mettewie was still being developed and the adjoining neighbourhoods were being parcelled and built up. This garden city, which is inspired by English neighbourhoods, with a network of small curved streets leading to squares and playgrounds, consists of single-family households and small apartment buildings. The houses were sold rather soon after they were built while the apartment buildings remained in hands of Logement Molenbeekois. The estate succeeds in striking a balance between the traditional style and the simplicity of Modernism. By using brick and a coating finish, gables with bull's eye windows, roofs with attic rooms, washed concrete lintels and consoles, loggias, wooden terraces and small bas-reliefs above each entrance, which symbolise the different continents, games, music instruments, the fables of de la Fontaine, the architect succeeded in adding variety and fantasy to his design...

◂ Cité Diongre

8/ CITÉ DE SAULNIER

RUE POTAERDEGAT AND RUE DES BÉGUINES AND AVENUE ARMAND DE SAULNIER, 1080 MOLENBEEK-SAINT-JEAN

Architect: Armand de Saulnier
Built: 1925-1926

In spite of a very tight budget, Armand de Saulnier presented plans for 99 dwellings along three streets that form a triangle with a garden in the centre. The architect joined forces with a company that used cheap building materials to build façades by combining aggregate concrete blocks that looked like stone and fired bricks. The design includes numerous triangular gables, bull's eye windows, small wooden entrances... The dwellings consisted of several apartments with a complex layout, with level differences and interconnected spaces. Each unit had its own front door, which explains why there are so many, usually in groups of three. Unfortunately, the budget constraints meant that there was no margin for decoration and the accommodation was very basic. Originally the dwellings were lit with petrol lamps, they had no bathroom and the WCs were located outside the dwellings. This lack of comfort did not seem to bother the first tenants who appreciated the cosy atmosphere and the neighbourhood's country feel. As of today, the complex is under heavy renovation.

◂ Cité De Saulnier (photo taken in 2014)

THE GARDEN CITIES

At the end of the nineteenth century, the British urban planner Ebenezer Howard wanted to solve the problem of densely-populated cities by building autonomous garden cities on the fringe. The garden cities of Letchworth (1904) and Hampstead (1905) in north London were subsequently built by the architects Raymond Unwin and Barry Parker. During World War I, several Belgian architects and urban planners, who were exiled in Great Britain or the Netherlands, defended the garden city model when asked for their opinion on how to rebuild the country. That is how the first housing typology to be implemented after the creation of the SNHLBM (1919) was that of the garden city. In Brussels, these are actually garden suburbs as these garden cities were never really fully autonomous. They were located on the fringe, where there was no land speculation. Due to a general lack of resources, the collective amenities that had been envisaged at the planning stage were never built, meaning these garden cities also depended on the city for everything. In Belgium, the garden cities were the result of an ideological compromise between Catholic ideas, which preferred individual housing and rural property, the liberal principles, which were founded on social segregation and the social ideals, which promoted urban, rented and shared housing. Soon the garden cities became expensive and as they could not fulfil demand, large tower blocks were built instead. Some critics felt that this was due to manipulation by political militants and feared Brussels would ultimately be encircled by a red belt!

The garden cities were built on the initiative of either tenants' cooperatives or local, parapublic companies. They paid special attention to their overall plans. The streets off the main thoroughfares were usually lined with single-family houses with a front garden. At the rear of the houses, the gardens gave out on footpaths, and sometimes on gardens of shared spaces. The initial layout of the housing was very rudimentary: the houses usually did not have a cellar, just a living room, a kitchen/laundry room and a toilet on the ground floor, with the bedrooms on the upper floor. The Brussels garden cities followed two major architectural trends:

1. The regionalist garden cities, which were inspired by the architecture of English cottages like La Roue (1921), in Anderlecht, where the first experiments were conducted with various low-cost construction techniques; Floréal (1920-1925) and Le Logis (1921-1927), in Watermael-Boitsfort, which were mainly designed and built by Jean-Jules Eggericx, an architect who spent the war years living in Britain;
2. More modernist garden cities: Cité Moderne (1922-1925), in Berchem-SainteAgathe, and Kapelleveld (1921-1927), in Woluwe-Saint-Lambert.

The road network of the more interesting garden cities was designed by Louis Van der Swaelmen (1883-1929), a theoretician and landscape designer who also lectured at La Cambre.

◥ Le Logis garden city, Watermael-Boitsfort, arch. J.-J. Eggericx, 1921-1927

◤▲ Floréal garden city, Watermael-Boitsfort, arch. J.-J. Eggericx, 1920-1925

9/ CITÉ MODERNE

PLACE DES COOPÉRATEURS AND SURROUND AREA, 1082 BERCHEM-SAINTE-AGATHE

Architect: Victor Bourgeois
Built: 1922-1925
Listed: 7/9/2000

Shortly after the construction of the Bovenhuis building Koekelberg, Victor Bourgeois undertook the construction of 275 dwellings on a 6-hectare plateau for the La Cité Moderne tenants' association. This garden city is the first large-scale example in Belgium of a Cubist, rational and standardised form of architecture. The absence of any ornamentation was designed to eliminate the social differences between the inhabitants. The utopian ideals which had the upper hand in this project are also reflected in the names of the streets and squares, which are called Entraide (solidarity), Évolution, Initiative, Bon Accueil (welcome)... The urban development, by Louis Van der Swaelmen, was organised in such a way to ensure the buildings benefited from maximum sunlight and to promote a sense of solidarity between the inhabitants. The short, interrupted streets, which were solely for local use, were combined with pedestrian pathways and meeting places, including small squares and gardens. There were 15 different types of houses, most of which were individual dwellings with two floors. The roofs are flat, except in certain streets near the city where they are pitched to ensure a seamless transition with the adjoining neighbourhoods. The entire garden city was built using lean concrete (a mix of industrial waste, sand and cement), which was poured in reusable formwork. This experimental method was both fast and cheap. Building a house took just twelve days: two for the assembly, two for the pouring of the concrete, five for the drying of the concrete, two for removing the formwork and one for unforeseen circumstances! Place des Coopérateurs is the centre of this garden city. Its two long sides are lined with dwellings that were built in a sawtooth pattern. A retail and apartment building, with three floors, which was recently restored, is the eye-catcher in the square. The staircases are clustered around the building's core and lit with large windows with abstract stained-glass windows, that are similar to the ones of Bovenhuis. These stained-glass windows were created by the painter Pierre-Louis Flouquet (1900-1967), who was a friend of the Bourgeois brothers, and also edited several architectural journals. Today the entire garden city needs restoring.

◀ La Cité Moderne, place des Coopérateurs ▶

TENANTS' COOPERATIVES

La Cité Moderne is one of the many tenants' associations to be established after the SNHLBM was founded in 1919. The tenants in these cooperatives underwrote part of the capital, while the State and the Province put up the rest. They are often linked to the flourishing trade unions, health insurance funds and cooperatives, recruiting their members in professional, cultural or intellectual circles. La Cité Moderne originated in Essor intellectual, an association of freethinkers, to which Victor Bourgeois belonged. Its founding members included 328 people, including employees, lower-ranked officials, municipal workers and so on, through articles and meetings. Tenants' cooperatives preferred the garden city housing model in the early Twenties.

The cooperatives mainly worked with modernist architects, whose progressive ideas they shared. Theoretically speaking, the tenants-cooperants had the opportunity to be part of the decision-making process about their new home and participate in the management of their city. Given the investment, which was relatively low, the cooperatives mainly attracted employees or financially well-off labourers. From 1923, the conservatives used this argument to limit their funding and thereby prevent the establishment of new cooperatives. Some of the cooperatives had to sell the housing that had already been built to continue operating.

10/ NATIONAL BASILICA OF THE SACRED HEART

1, PARVIS DE LA BASILIQUE, 1083 GANSHOREN AND 1081 KOEKELBERG

Architects: Albert Van huffel and then Paul Rome

Built: 1926-1971

The basilica stands out because of its impressive size. At the time that it was built, it was the world's second largest building. King Leopold II had the idea to build a church that would be larger than Sacré-Coeur in Paris, at the top of boulevard Léopold II. As the State refused to fund the project, the king turned to the Church for assistance, obtaining the founding of the Parish of the Sacred Heart. It tasked the architect Pierre Langerock with the construction of a neo-Gothic basilica. The king attended the stone-laying ceremony in 1905. Only the foundation was completed when war broke out.

In 1920, Cardinal Mercier was eager to continue building the basilica, albeit at a lesser cost, dedicating the building to the liberation of the country and to the soldiers killed in combat. That is why a competition was organised, with every architect in Belgium invited to participate. There was no winner, which is why the architect Albert Van huffel (1877-1935) was tasked with the largest ever building commission in Belgium of a religious building, on a simple recommendation. This was a huge undertaking for a self-taught architect, who did not participate in the competition and who never

▼ National Basilica of the Sacred Heart

▶ Nave of the National Basilica of the Sacred Heart

built a church. His previous projects included dwellings in Ghent and a casino in Middelkerke.
What's more, Van huffel was affiliated with the socialist party! The project's scale model, which was presented at the International Exhibition of Decorative and Industrial Arts in Paris in 1925, won the Grand Prix of Architecture. The works started in 1926 and progressed gradually. The old foundations were replaced with 1,438 concrete piles cast in Franki concrete (after the name of its Liège-based inventor, Edgard Frankignoul). From 1930, Van huffel collaborated with Paul Rome (1896-1989), who continued the project single-handedly after 1935. The basilica was completed in 1971. This building is a real manifesto of religious Art Deco. The interior volumes have remarkable proportions. The building's reinforced concrete structure was concealed in the basilica with facing bricks and terracotta, creating a warmer, yellowish interior. *Terracotta is a ceramic product which can be used as formwork for concrete. It consists of hollow blocks, which are enamelled in the oven and installed before the concrete. The concrete is then poured into these blocks, melding with the structure.*[2]

Do walk up to just below the dome, for a panoramic view from the exterior gallery where you can enjoy one of the best views of Brussels.

At 25, avenue Jacques Sermon, you will find an imposing house with a garage and outbuildings in an L shape (arch. Antoine Pompe, 1922).
Its rustic yet comfortable appearance is emphasised by its pitched roof, the tall chimneys, a loggia with a triangular gable, and a timbered design. Here the architect chose to highlight the contrasts between colours and materials, combining a white-rendered beige stone, dark wood and red roof tiles.
The entrance is surmounted by a stone panel with birds and some of the corners, especially those of the loggia, are accentuated with wooden elements, carved with geometric and anthropomorphic shapes. While Pompe preached a rational design, his architecture was rather sentimental, using traditional materials.

▼ Dwelling, 25, av. J. Sermon, arch. A. Pompe

11/ WITHUIS

183, AVENUE CHARLES WOESTE, 1090 JETTE

Architect: Joseph Diongre
Built: 1927
Listed: 25/2/1985

While working on the garden city project that was named after him, Joseph Diongre met Jef Mennekens, the municipal secretary of Molenbeek, who was also a poet and a writer and who asked him to design him a home. Mennekens, who liked modern designs, accepted Diongre's rather bold design, which combined modernist elements (rooftop terrace, horizontal windows...) with Art Deco. The façade's rhythm is all about recessed and protruding volumes, making it look almost like a Cubist house, with open and closed surfaces. The design combines the symmetry of the upper floors with an asymmetric ground floor. The front door is on the right. The diagonal staircase that connects the entrance with the pavement connects the symmetry with the asymmetry. On the ground floor, the inscription Withuis accentuates the house's central axis. The letters JM for Jef Mennekens, in the same font, form the small grate in front of the peephole in the front door. On either side of the staircase, the tubular garden fence features two decorative elements: one with the house number, the other featuring a pen and an inkwell to remind everyone that this was the house of an author. The wine-red and green window frames, doors, garden fences and railings of the terraces create a fun contrast with the white granito of the façade. The house has always remained in the family, which is why the interior has been so well preserved. This is a gesamtkunstwerk as Diongre also designed part of the furniture.

At 175, rue Firmin Lecharlier, Diongre built a house with a brick façade, with protruding elements that are accentuated by bands of bricks that were lacquered a rich wine red and green. The colours are similar to the colours used for the doors and windows of Withuis. The windows and the frames add an original twist to this façade, which is inscribed with the date of its construction (1927) in an Art Deco font.

◂ Withuis

JOSEPH DIONGRE (1878-1963)

After studying design and architecture at the Academy of Brussels and several work placements, Diongre travelled to the Netherlands to study architecture. He was quite impressed with the work of H. P. Berlage, one of the first followers of functionalism, adopting his penchant for abstract volumes in his designs.

Before World War I, Diongre built several houses for the upper middle class in a variety of styles, ranging from the neo-Renaissance to Art Nouveau. During the interwar period, his work was more eclectic. He built several affordable dwellings in Saint-Gilles, Laeken and mainly Molenbeek, in a style that veered between moderate Modernism, Art Deco and regionalism.

His private dwellings are usually designed in a pared down Art Deco style, more rarely in the modernist style. There is one exception, however: his Cubist-inspired Withuis, with its bold combination of rendered volumes.

The friendship between Diongre and Jef Mennekens, the municipal secretary of Molenbeek, explains why the architect built so many houses in this municipality. His participation in several competitions also led him to build the monumental modernist town hall of Woluwe-Saint-Lambert (1935-1939) and, in 1935-1938, the National Radio Broadcasting Institute in Ixelles.

12/ CITÉ DUBRUCQ

184-198, AVENUE JEAN DUBRUCQ, 1080 MOLENBEEK-SAINT-JEAN

Architect: Adolphe Puissant
Built: 1921-1922

We now walk through the maritime quarter, which was urbanised in the early twentieth century, when the warehouse, the ferry terminal and the Tour and Taxis customs buildings were built. Many businesses and shops moved in, leading to the construction of housing for the many workers they employed. After World War I, Le Logement Molenbeekois built several tower blocks here. These two groups of U-shaped apartment buildings were constructed around the shared garden on the street side. The façades have terraces and combine rendered and exposed bricks and brick reliefs. The front doors are decorated with ironwork, featuring tools including a hammer, pliers, a square... As an architect consultant to the SNHLBM, Adolphe Puissant (1878-1950) travelled to Britain, Germany and the Netherlands to study architectural solutions there before building a series of worker's cities.

Nearby, at 201-205 and 209 avenue Jean Dubrucq, 45-47 rue François Mus and 36-42 rue Gabrielle Petit, Joseph Diongre built a series of apartment buildings around a shared inner court, from 1921 until 1923, using his typical architectural vocabulary including rendered surfaces, relief brickwork, triangular or rectangular balconies with openwork masonry railings, washed concrete lintels and consoles for the balconies... The entrance span of the buildings all feature a bas-relief, with different motifs. The layout of the units was very simple. The rent depended on the number of rooms and the floor on which the unit was situated as there was no lift.

▼ Cité Dubrucq

13/ ANCIENS ÉTABLISSEMENTS GOSSET

6, RUE GABRIELLE PETIT, 1080 MOLENBEEK-SAINT-JEAN

Architect: Adrien Blomme
Built: 1929

At the end of the Twenties, the Gosset cigarette factory, which is better known for its Saint-Michel brand, built new buildings for its many, large machines. Adrien Blomme built an Art Deco ensemble, with a reinforced concrete structure, that looked both functional and interesting on the visual level.

In 1990, the Brussels Regional Development Agency (citydev.brussels) acquired the premises entrusting Joël Claisse with its renovation. Nowadays, citydev.brussels has its offices here, sharing the buildings with small and medium-sized companies like bx1 (a local TV channel).

◂ Anciens établissements Gosset

You will easily recognise a series of dwellings built by Diongre on the corner of rue de l'Escaut (81-87) and rue de Rotterdam (9-13), which date from the same period as the dwellings in avenue Dubrucq. These dwellings were intended for families who lived in the slums. The terraces created a sense of privacy while allowing them to maintain the relationship with their neighbours that they were accustomed to.

At the top of rue de Rotterdam, a small public space overlooks the Tour and Taxis site. It was gradually abandoned in the Eighties, after which it was the subject of some speculation. It is currently undergoing a full reconversion, making way for a new, fully sustainable neighbourhood. The renovated warehouses are home to shops, offices and are used for events.

At 75-89, rue du Laekenveld, Cité Laekenveld, which was built in 1921-1923 by Armand de Saulnier, is the predecessor of the city which the architect subsequently built near boulevard Mettewie. The gabled roofs with their bull's eye windows are a typical feature of his style. Here he also started to experiment with the aggregate concrete blocks that imitate natural stone and which in a sense became his trademark.

This visit, which was inspired by the history of social housing, ends with a lovely Art Deco town house, on the corner of boulevard du Jubilé (86-88) and rue Henri Hollevoet, by Jean-Baptiste Dewin. The house was built in 1927 for the owner of the Compagnie industrielle du Rupel, which produced bricks and tiles. He installed his office there, and lived there himself. The company must have owned warehouses along the canal which explains the presence of its offices in this quarter. Today the building is owned by an insurance company that has carefully restored it.

◣ Cité Laekenveld, 75-89, rue du Laekenveld, arch. A. De Saulnier

◢ Town house, 86-88, bd du Jubilée, arch. J.-B. Dewin

AND MORE...

SOME READING AND FILM TITLES TO FIND OUT MORE ABOUT THE ARCHITURE OF THE INTERWAR PERIOD

- Ayn Rand, *The Fountainhead*, 1943: a captivating novel, inspired by the life of Frank Lloyd Wright, about an architect who refuses to adhere to historical convention and classical style in building design. The novel, which is also a wonderful love story, elaborates on the conflict between the traditionalists and modernists in architecture. A film, based on the book, was released in 1949, starring Gary Cooper and directed by King Vidor.

- Two romanticised biographies of Frank Lloyd Wright were recently published:
  - T. C. Boyle, *The Women*, 2010
  - Nancy Horan, *Loving Frank*, 2009

- Éric De Kuyper, *Je viendrai comme un voleur*, 1994. A psychological thriller that takes place in the Residence Palace. A great way of discovering this building, which has been irretrievably altered since then...

- Robert Vivier, *Folle qui s'ennuie*, 1933. This novel takes place in the garden city of Logis-Floréal and describes the daily life of a family of members of a housing cooperative. Above all, it tells the story of young, quiet Antonia, whose stifling and boring life leads her to a desire for change...

- Kate Milie, *L'assassin aime l'Art Déco*, 2012. This thriller unfolds against the Art Deco buildings of Brussels.

- *L'Inhumaine*, a French film by Marcel L'Herbier, 1923. This silent film tells the story of a famous singer who rejects the advances of her admirers. A young scientist commits suicide, consumed by his passion for her. The film is mainly extraordinary because of the sets, which were designed by Robert Mallet-Stevens and Fernand Léger!

- *Metropolis*, a German film by Fritz Lang, 1927. This science fiction film unfolds against the backdrop of a futuristic urban dystopia, called Metropolis, where a caste of privileged factory owners exploits slaves who dwell in the underground under the city and who must work to the insane rhythm of the machines that operate the city. The magnificent sets are a reminder that Fritz Lang, who was the son of a Viennese architect, originally wanted to become an architect himself!

- Finally, to get a better idea of the atmosphere of the interwar period, we also suggest reading the books of Irène Némirovsky, F. Scott Fitzgerald, William Somerset Maugham... or watching *Hercule Poirot* (1989-2013), a British TV series in which David Suchet plays the role of the idiosyncratic Belgian detective.

PLACES TO VISIT

❋ **David and Alice van Buuren Museum**
41, avenue Léo Errera
1180 Brussels
www.museumvanbuuren.be

❋ **The Clockarium – The Museum of Art Deco ceramic clock**
163, boulevard Reyers
1030 Brussels
www.clockarium.be

❋ **Villa Empain – The Boghossian Foundation**
67, avenue Franklin Roosevelt
1050 Bruxelles
www.villaempain.com

❋ **Villa Clairval – Lussato Institute**
52-54, avenue de la Sapinière
1180 Brussels
www.brunolussatoinstitute.be

❋ **Flagey**
27, rue du Belvédère
1050 Brussels
www.flagey.be

❋ **Centre for Fine Arts**
23, rue Ravenstein
1000 Brussels
www.bozar.be

❋ **Basilica of the Sacred Heart**
1, parvis de la Basilique
1083 Brussels
www.basilicakoekelberg.be

❋ **KANAL – Centre Pompidou**
quai des Péniches
1000 Brussels
http://kanal.brussels

HERITAGE PROTECTION AND AWARENESS

❋ **Interbellum asbl**
Association for research about the renewed creativity during the interwar period
69, Olijfstraat
9000 Ghent
www.interbellum.org

❋ **DOCOMOMO Belgium asbl**
Association that promotes the documentation and conservation of modernist heritage while bringing together experts and amateurs of this genre of architecture.
www.docomomo.be

❋ **Directorate of Monuments and Sites**
Ministry of the Brussels-Capital Region
1035 Brussels
www.patrimoine.brussels

❋ **homegrade.brussels**
7, place Quetelet
1210 Brussels
http://homegrade.brussels

❋ ***Les Nouvelles du Patrimoine***
Journal of the Association of the Friends of UNESCO in Belgium
29/63, rue Émile Steeno
1160 Brussels
www.nouvellesdupatrimoine.be

GUIDED VISITS AND EVENTS

❋ **Cécile Dubois**
cecile8968@hotmail.com
Phone: + 32 (0)478 229 228

❋ **Brussels Art Deco Society**
Evoking the period from the Twenties to the Forties in Brussels and the surrounding region with talks, guided tours, festive events...
brusselsartdecosociety@hotmail.com
https://www.facebook.com/Brussels-Art-Deco-Society-1056202227762614/

❋ **Explore.brussels**
www.explore.brussels
The umbrella organisation of ARAU, Arkadia, Brussels Chatterguides and Pro Velo organises the Brussels Art Nouveau & Art Deco Festival (BANAD festival).

❋ **Festival ARTONOV ASBL**
www.festival-artonov.eu
Interdisciplinary festival (music, dance, theatre, visual arts and fashion) inspired by Art Nouveau and Art Deco

WEBSITES

Inventory of the architectural heritage of the Brussels-Capital Region and registers of listed buildings:
www.irismonument.be

Pierre Dangles, biography of architects who worked in the "Pierres Précieuses" neighbourhood (where the streets are named after precious stones) in Schaerbeek:
www.opale-opaal.be/architectes-ayant-oeuvre-dans-le-quartier

DOCUMENTATION CENTRE

CIVA – https://civa.brussels
The CIVA develops a large number of activities and services including temporary and permanent exhibitions, talks, educational activities and events. Its archives and library collections, comprising just under 40,000 publications and journals on architecture, urban planning, the history of cities, landscape, gardens and urban ecosystems, are open to the public.

BIBLIOGRAPHY

Archives consulted by the author

- The archives of the urban planning departments of the City of Brussels, Ixelles and Uccle

Journals consulted by the author

- *Bâtir* – monthly magazine – Brussels, 1932-1940
- *La Cité* – monthly magazine – Brussels, 1919-1935
- *Clarté* – monthly magazine – Brussels, 1927-1939
- *L'Émulation* – monthly magazine – Brussels, 1921-1939
- *L'Époque* – periodical – Brussels, 1933-1939/40
- *La Revue documentaire* – monthly magazine – Brussels, 1931-1933
- *La Technique des Travaux* – monthly magazine – Liège, 1925-1940

Contemporary journals consulted by the author

- *Les Nouvelles du Patrimoine*, Brussels
- *Bulletins de Pétitions-Patrimoine*, Brussels

General works on architecture and the decorative arts in Brussels and Belgium

- *Académie de Bruxelles. Deux siècles d'architecture*, AAM, Brussels, 1989
- ARON J., PUTTEMANS P., BURNIAT P., *L'architecture moderne à Bruxelles. Guide*, Octogone, Brussels, 1996
- *Art et architecture publics*, Brussels-Capital Region-Mardaga, Brussels-Sprimont, 1999
- BIVER I., *Cinémas de Bruxelles. Portraits et destins*, CFC-Éditions, Brussels, 2009
- Collectif, *Le patrimoine monumental de la Belgique. Bruxelles. Volume 1*, 3 tomes, Mardaga, Liège, 1989-1994
- DE HENS G. and MARTINY V.-G., *Académie Royale des Beaux-Arts de Bruxelles, une école d'architecture, des tendances*, Société Populaire d'Éditions, Brussels, 1992
- *Ensembles architecturaux en Région bruxelloise*, Région de Bruxelles-Capitale – Racine, Brussels, 1997
- *Itinéraire du patrimoine résidentiel bruxellois*, Royal Belgian Geographical Society, Brussels, 2007 (Collection Hommes et Paysages, No 38-39)
- LEBLANC CL. (dir.), *Art Nouveau & Design. Les arts décoratifs de 1830 à l'Expo 58*, Racine, Brussels, 2005
- *Monuments et Sites protégés 1998-2003*, La Renaissance du Livre/Brussels-Capital Region, Tournai-Brussels, 2003
- *Musée des AAM. Collections, T.I*, AAM, Brussels, 1986
- VAN LOO A. (dir.), *Dictionnaire de l'architecture en Belgique de 1830 à nos jours*, Mercator Fund, Antwerp, 2003

Works on the interwar period in Brussels and Belgium

- *Bruxelles Art Déco. 1920-1930*, Norma, Paris, 1996
- CALTAGIRONE S., BREYDEL L.-PH., *Intérieurs Bruxellois. Modernisme & Art Déco*, Alice, Brussels, 2004
- CULOT M. and TERLINDEN FR., *Antoine Pompe et l'effort moderne en Belgique. 1890-1940*, Éditions du Musée d'Ixelles, Brussels, 1969
- DELHAYE J., *L'appartement d'aujourd'hui*, Éditions Desoer, Liège, undated
- *Guide de l'Architecture des Années 25 à Bruxelles*, AAM, Brussels, 1983
- *Modernisme Art Déco*, Brussels-Capital Region-Mardaga, Brussels-Sprimont, 2004

Works about a specific architect or building

- ANSPACH I., *Musée et jardins van Buuren*, Mercator Fund/Van Buuren Museum, Brussels, 2007
- AUBRY FR., *Horta ou la passion de l'architecture*, Ludion, Gent, 2005
- Collectif, *La villa Empain. Histoire et restauration*, Brussels-Capital Region/ Boghossian Foundation, Brussels, 2009
- CORDEIRO P., *Sacraal Beton. De Sint-Augustinuskerk te Vorst*, in Monumenten en Landschappen, May-June 1994, p. 41-56

- CULOT M. and PIRLOT A.-M., *Antoine Courtens. Créateur Art Déco*, AAM, Brussels, 2002
- BLOMME FR., *À la rencontre d'Adrien Blomme 1878-1940, sa vie son œuvre*, CIVA, Brussels, 2004
- Collectif, *Brunfaut's progressive architecture*, CFC-Éditions, Brussels, 2013
- Collectif, *Henry van de Velde. Passion, Fonction, Beauté*, Lannoo, Tielt, 2013
- FONTAINE J., *La maison de verre. Paul-Amaury Michel*, AAM, Brussels, 2004
- HENNAUT E., *La Prévoyance Sociale. Histoire et restauration.* Bruxelles, AAM, Brussels, 2004
- HENNAUT E., *La Loge. Du temple au musée*, AAM, Brussels, 2002
- HORTA V., *Mémoires*, Ministry of the French Community, Brussels, 1985
- LEBLANC PH., *Le Palais de la Folle Chanson / architecte Antoine Courtens, Étude et proposition de restauration*, Université libre de Bruxelles, Brussels, 1999 (Master's thesis)
- *Louis Herman De Koninck. Architecte des Années Modernes*, AAM, Brussels, 1998
- PLOEGAERTS L., PUTTEMANS P., *L'œuvre architecturale de Henry van de Velde*, Atelier Vokaer – Les Presses de l'Université Laval, Brussels-Québec, 1987
- SCHOONBROODT, B., *Michel Polak, de l'Art nouveau à l'Art Déco*, CEBO, Brussels, 2003
- *Renaissance d'un monument,* SD WORX, Brussels, undated
- STRAUWEN I., *Les frères Bourgeois, architecture et plastique pure*, AAM, Brussels, 2005
- VANDENBREEDEN J. and VAN SANTVOORT L., *Joseph Diongre. Architecte*, Sint-Lukasarchief-Plaizier, Brussels, 1989

Social housing and the garden cities

- *3000 Foyers Bruxellois*, Le Foyer Bruxellois S.C. – Les dossiers de La Fonderie, Brussels, 1997
- *Bruxelles, 150 ans de logements ouvriers et sociaux*, Dire, Brussels, 1989
- *Cités-jardins 1920-1940 en Belgique*, AAM, Brussels, 1994
- Cooparch–RU, *Les sites remarquables du patrimoine social bruxellois*, Société du Logement de la Région bruxelloise, Brussels, 2000
- HUBERTY C., *Le Logement Molenbeekois : une histoire de société*, Le Logement Molenbeekois, Brussels, 1999
- *Décider de son logement. L'habitat coopératif à Bruxelles*, "Les Cahiers de La Fonderie", special issue, Brussels, 1993
- SMETS M., *L'avènement de la cité-jardin en Belgique. Histoire de l'habitat social en Belgique de 1830 à 1930*, Mardaga, Brussels-Liège, 1977

INDEX OF ARCHITECTS AND ARTISTS

The pages with the most complete biographical information are indicated in bold.

NOTES

introduction

Patrick Burniat, *Habiter Moderne*, in *Modernisme et Art Déco*, Mardaga – Brussels-Capital Region, Sprimont-Brussels, 2004, p. 55.

walk 1

1. Grégoire Ch., *Résidence Belle-Vue*, in *Clarté*, May 1937, p. VII-IX.
2. Ploegaerts L. and Puttemans P., *L'œuvre architecturale de Henry van de Velde*, Atelier Vokaer – Les Presses de l'Université de Laval, Brussels-Québec, 1987, p. 191.
3. Quote of A. Blomme in an article by Ch. Imbert, *La maison d'un architecte, 52 avenue des Nations*, in *La Technique des Travaux*, No. 8, August 1931, p. 471-482.
4. Idem.
5. AVB/TP 354.54 (1928).

walk 2

1. Van Everbroeck L., *90 appartements !...*, in *Bâtir*, No. 49, December 1936, p. 965.
2. Excerpt from a letter sent by the Agnès company to the City of Brussels as part of the permit granting process - AVB/TP 46993 (1931).

walk 3

1. Horta V., *Mémoires*, Ministry of the French Community, Brussels, 1985, p. 243.
2. Katzarova D., *Le bâtiment de la RVS : renaissance ou réminiscence ?*, in *Les Nouvelles du Patrimoine*, No. 77, July-August-September 1998, p. 27-28.

walk 4

1. Flouquet P.-L., *Une habitation solaire*, in *Bâtir*, No. 46, 1936, p. 845-846.
2. Flouquet P.-L., *Claire Maison à Bruxelles*, in *Bâtir*, No. 42, May 1936, p. 667-668.

walk 5

1. Puttemans R., *La terrasse et l'ornement dans l'architecture moderne*, in *Clarté*, No. 3, 1931, p. 1-2.

walk 6

1. Huberty C., *Le Logement Molenbeekois : une histoire de société*, Le Logement Molenbeekois, Brussels, 1999, p. 26-31.
2. Novgorodsky L., *La Basilique nationale du Sacré-Cœur à Bruxelles*, in *La Technique des Travaux*, No. 5, May 1938, p. 241-257.

PHOTO CREDITS

Photographies Sophie Voituron – **www.sophie-voituron.com**

except:

Cécile Dubois : pages 26, 76, 153 (left).

© Le Plaza Hotel Brussels: page 90.

© Sofam 2018:
Joseph Diongre: pages 25, 146, 151, 154, 163.

© SABAM 2018:
Henry van de Velde: pages 37 and 136.

Every reasonable effort has been made to trace the holders of the copyright to the illustrations, in accordance with legal requirements. Copyright holders whom we were unable to locate are requested to contact the publisher.

Cover caption:
Top: Villa Empain / Boghossian Foundation
Bottom: A. and D. van Buuren Museum

Text: Cécile Dubois
Translation from French: Sandy Logan
Proofreading: Karine Leroux
Photos: Sophie Voituron

Graphic design and maps:
Aikaterini Chronopoulou **www.aika-design.com**

This book is published by Éditions Racine.
Éditions Racine is part of the Lannoo Publishing Group.
For more information:
www.lannoo.be
www.racine.be
Subscribe to our newsletter and receive regular updates about our latest publications and activities.

Tour et Taxis, Entrepôt royal
86C, avenue du Port, BP 104A • B - 1000 Brussels

D. 2018, 6852. 25
Legal deposit: October 2018
ISBN 978-2-39025-058-6